Enjoy!

AnBegieneman

THE
SI PETERSON
STORY

A Legacy of Faith

by Si's Mom — Anita Begieneman

 **FriesenPress**

Suite 300 - 990 Fort St
Victoria, BC, Canada, V8V 3K2
www.friesenpress.com

Copyright © 2015 by Anita Begieneman
First Edition — 2015

ISBN
978-1-4602-4017-5 (Hardcover)
978-1-4602-4018-2 (Paperback)
978-1-4602-4019-9 (eBook)

1. Biography & Autobiography, Personal Memoirs

Distributed to the trade by The Ingram Book Company

Table of Contents

Acknowledgments

My gratitude goes out to the following people, without whose help and encouragement I would never have been able to write Si's story.

My heart-felt thanks to

- my daughter Leigh Ann, my sons David and Ben, my foster son Kent Richardson, and my good friend John Livingston, for all the assistance they gave me in so many different areas.

- my husband Marinus and all my family for their faith in my abilities and for their encouragement every step of the way.

- Dana Mills and all the wonderful people at FriesenPress. I could not have asked for a more patient and encouraging publishing team.

DEDICATION

This book is dedicated to all the wonderful people whose love and caring concern for Si, made his life complete.

"You cannot behold with your natural eyes, for the present time, the design of your God concerning those things which shall come hereafter, and the glory which shall follow after much tribulation.

For after much tribulation come the blessings."

Doctrine and Covenants 58:3-4

Introduction

This is the story of an extraordinary person who lived an extraordinary life. This is the story of my son, Frank Siedel Peterson (Si)

On March 1, 1975, Si fell from a high bar while doing gymnastics, and broke his neck at the first cervical vertabrae. He was instantly and totally paralyzed from his chin down. He was 16 years of age at the time and he spent the next 18 years (the whole rest of his life) as a complete quadriplegic, unable to breathe on his own, talk out loud, or even turn his own head.

Others have suffered similar trials, but what makes Si's life so extraordinary is the way he lived it — with courage, faith, and complete trust in his Heavenly Father's will.

I have procrastinated writing this book because of fear that I would not be able to capture the essence of his remarkable life and spirit in mere words, but the promptings I received to write it would not go away. In fact one day, as I was thinking about it, it was as if Si was standing beside me and I heard him say to me "Come on mom — just do it!"

And so I let my faith overcome my trepidation and I began…

I'm not sure if it is possible for a mother to be completely objective when she writes about her child, but I have endeavoured to write as accurately as I could, and I have felt the Spirit with me as I have written. I pray that, as you read, your spirits will be touched, and you will be able to *feel* the things I may not have been able to adequately express.

Most of the events recorded in this book were taken from Si's journals and from my own journals. Whatever is taken from Si's journals will be in italics.

There may be some of you, who read this story, that may not be familiar with the terminology and the doctrine of The Church of

Jesus Christ of Latter-day Saints, the church that Si and his family are members of. You may find it helpful to go to our church's official web site which is www.lds.org to find answers to any questions you may have.

People have often said to me that after they met Si, they could never forget him. Because many of you did not have the opportunity to meet him, I would like to introduce him to you.

Si was the oldest of my six children. His five younger siblings, at the time of his accident, (March 1, 1975) were Lori - 15, David - 14, Leigh Ann - 12, Benjie - 8, and Barbie - 6. His father, Frank Peterson, and I were divorced on February 15, 1975, two weeks before Si's accident happened, and his half sister Trish, Frank's daughter, was born two weeks after.

Si was baptized at the age of eight and was an active member of the Church of Jesus Christ of Latter-day Saints. He was an average student in school. He was a good athlete and loved all sports, especially volleyball. He was an accomplished pianist who played by ear and by note. He was an exceptional artist. He was a tease who loved to play practical jokes, especially on me. He was quite tall. By the age of 16, he was over 6 feet tall. He had many friends and was well liked by his peers. I guess you could say he was a typical teenager.

His only sort of long-term goal was to attend Brigham Young University in Provo, Utah for a year after high school, to prepare to serve a mission for his church when he turned nineteen.

But our Heavenly Father had a different plan for Si's life…

Si, age 16, a few months before his accident.

1

"THE THIRTY SECONDS THAT CHANGED MY LIFE"

It was on a Saturday morning in March, when my world suddenly changed. I woke up late that morning for volleyball practice and thought to myself, "I'm late, but who cares! I'm too tired to rush!"

As I slowly got dressed, I listened to CHED, my favourite radio station. After I finished dressing, I turned off my radio and walked out into the cool spring air. I jogged the four blocks to Avalon Junior High School where the practice was being held. When I got there, I changed into my gym clothes, warmed up, and then began spiking practice with the other guys.

Volleyball is my favourite sport. I enjoyed practicing — especially because my Dad was the coach. He made the practices enjoyable with different kinds of drills and routines and he expected us to work hard. Because I wanted to be the best volleyball player I could be, I really listened to what my Dad told me to do and tried hard to put these skills into my playing. We had a good volleyball team and there was a good feeling among the members.

We practiced for about 3 hours and then my Dad, my brother David and most of the guys left. Three of my team mates, two Mormon Missionaries from the Bonnie Doon Stake (who had never been to our practice before) and I stayed to shoot some baskets. Usually just my brother David and I stayed after practice. This change in our usual routine was to prove very significant in the events that followed that morning.

After we got tired of shooting baskets, my friends and I set up the high bar to practice some gymnastics. Little did I know how much this one act was going to change my life.

We took turns doing different routines and when it came my turn I decided to try a particular dismount that I had seen one of my friends do in gym class.

It is a relatively simple dismount called a cherry-drop. I had tried it before but wanted to do it again to see if I could improve it.

I took a couple of practice swings hanging from my knees. When I went back and out I was supposed to let my legs slide from the bar and land on my feet, but I think my feet got caught on the bar and I fell to the floor, landing on the back of my head instead.

Instantly I heard a loud ringing sound, and when I tried to roll over and get up I couldn't move. When I tried to take a breath I found I couldn't breathe. I tried to call for help, but I couldn't speak. I laid there, trying to figure out what was happening, because nothing would work for me. I got really scared!

My friends thought I was fooling around and they called to me to get up. After a few minutes, when I still hadn't moved, they came over to see what was wrong. They rolled me over and I tried to tell them I wasn't breathing but no sound came out of my mouth. I was trying to speak so quickly that I am sure they could not have read my lips, but somehow the Lord made known to them that I was really in trouble and couldn't breathe. They started giving me mouth to mouth resuscitation. One ran to call an ambulance, and the Missionaries blessed me that I would be calm and be able to reach the hospital in safety, where I could receive the help I needed. When the ambulance arrived on the scene, the drivers were amazed at how calm and in control everything was.

Someone called my Dad and he came back to the school and rode with me in the ambulance to the hospital.

I know now that my Dad was very aware of the seriousness of the situation, but he put on a good front and told me jokes all the way to the hospital.

The events of that Saturday morning in March are part of my Heavenly Father's plan for my life, and because He knew they were going to happen, He made sure there were people available to do the things that would be necessary in order to preserve my life.

A miracle had occurred; the first of many that I would eventually experience!

Yes, the Si Peterson Story is a story of miracles, but it is also, a story of courage and faith — a faith so strong that miracles were a natural outcome of that faith. The miracles and the faith required to bring them about are so intertwined that one is left to wonder which came first.

This is a story of miracles that I hope will leave a legacy of faith.

2

THE DIAGNOSIS

I had been asked to give a workshop at the Bonnie Doon Stake's Youth Conference that was to be held in Red Deer on March 1, 1975. I had asked two of my children, Si and Lori, who were old enough to attend the conference, if they would like to go with me. Lori readily accepted but Si declined because he was part of a dance number that was to perform at our Stake Dance Festival. He didn't want to miss the practice that afternoon. I remember going into our family room the night before, seeing Si lying on the floor in front of the TV, and thinking what a beautiful young man he had grown into. I felt so blessed to have him for my son, and I shall always remember the warmth and love I felt toward him in that moment.

Lori and I travelled safely from Edmonton to Red Deer that Saturday morning and I had completed two workshops before the lunch hour. We had just finished lunch when someone came running up to me and said that I was to call home. I immediately felt very apprehensive because I knew my children would not disturb me at a conference unless something serious had happened at home. I was shaking so badly that I could hardly dial the numbers. David answered the phone and said that Si had had an accident and that I should come home right away because he had been taken to the hospital.

Lori and I quickly gathered up my workshop materials, I explained the situation to the Young Women's President who was in charge of the Conference, and then we ran for the car.

I was driving a Chrysler Station Wagon and it had a very powerful engine. As soon as we were on the highway, I floored it hoping that the RCMP would stop me for speeding and escort me to Edmonton, but there was not one in sight. There was, however, a person driving on the highway that thought I wanted to have a race with him. He would pass me going about a hundred miles an hour, pull in front of me and then slow down. I would then pass him and he would do the same thing again. I had no way of telling him that I was in an emergency situation and not just speeding for the fun of it. His behaviour was very dangerous and extremely nerve racking, but Lori said a fervent prayer and we reached the University Hospital in safety.

I didn't know where to park so we left the car in the Emergency entrance and ran into the hospital. I asked the receptionist where they had taken Si Peterson and she directed me to a small room. When we entered the room we found a doctor sitting behind a desk. Frank and our Home Teachers, Dean Hunt and Ron Davidson, were sitting in chairs in front of him. Lori and I sat down and the doctor proceeded to tell us that Si was completely paralyzed from his chin down and, if he lived, would never walk again or breathe on his own again. This was too much for me to hear and I asked him to stop. He did, and we sat there in stunned silence. After I had composed myself I asked him if Si would recover and he didn't answer me. Frank asked him if he had heard my question and he said yes but that I had told him to stop talking. His seeming insensitivity to me was very hurtful. Frank then asked him to please answer my question.

He then told us the details of Si's very serious injuries. As I sat there trying to comprehend what I had just been told, I began to realize what this would mean in our lives. I felt an overwhelming feeling that I would not be able to do what would be required of me. For a brief moment it was as if my Heavenly Father completely withdrew His Spirit from me and I was left totally and completely alone. I became acutely aware of the magnitude of the responsibility that was placed upon me. I cannot describe in words the feeling of helplessness, inadequacy and despair that I felt. Then, it was as if my Heavenly Father put His arms around me and I felt a peaceful, warm assurance that I didn't have to do it alone — that He would always be there with me to help me.

My Home Teachers gave me a blessing so that I would be calm when I saw Si, and be able to be a source of strength and comfort to him.

They then took me to see my son.

He was in a room, the only other occupant being a small baby in a crib. It was an Intensive Care Unit. Si was lying on his back, wide awake, and had a hose coming out of his mouth that was attached to a large machine. I realized that the machine was a respirator and that it was breathing for him. I stood taking in the scene before me, and then crossed the room to my beautiful son.

We looked at each other for a moment and then Si tried to tell me something. Because of the tubing in his mouth he could not form the words well enough for me to be able to read his lips. After several minutes of trying and not succeeding I thought of a plan. I told Si that I would say the alphabet and when I got to the right letter he was to blink his eyes once and if it was wrong he was to blink twice. It was slow going but he finally spelled out the word "glass". I immediately thought he wanted a glass of something to drink so I asked him if that was what he wanted. He blinked twice. I stood there really perplexed for a few minutes and then I asked him if there was more to the word and he blinked once. I started through the alphabet again and finally realized that he wanted his glasses. I found his glasses and put them on him. A look of relief came over his face, not just because he could see better, but more because of the realization that we had finally found a way to communicate with each other.

I phoned my sister Eltie, who lived in Raymond, and she phoned my Mom and Dad to tell them what had happened. They left immediately to come to Edmonton to be with me. They arrived around midnight. My sister is a nurse and I thought that everything would be better when she got there — that she would be able to take the heavy responsibilities I felt, from me. But I soon realized that people could comfort me and help me, but they could not take upon themselves the responsibilities that were mine.

A female doctor asked me to come out into the hall. She spoke to me about the quality of life Si would have if he lived, and then she said to me, "I hope you realize that there are worse things than dying."

Our Relief Society President, June Carter, and her husband, Darwin, came up to the hospital as soon as they heard, and stayed with me throughout the night. What a source of strength and comfort they were to me.

Si was transferred to a respiratory Intensive Care Unit (ICU) the following day, and I felt a measure of comfort knowing he would be in more experienced hands.

About noon that day I went home from the hospital to get a little rest and to get cleaned up. When I got home, I went down into Si's room and sat on his bed and cried out to my Heavenly Father, "Why? Why did this terrible thing happen to my beautiful young son?!" As I sat there crying and questioning, thoughts began to form in my mind and I knew that Heavenly Father was speaking to me through the Holy Ghost. He was seeking to comfort me. I quickly grabbed a pen and some paper from Si's desk and wrote the words as they came into my mind.

"This life is a training ground for Godhood. How we meet the trials that come and how we let them affect our lives are very important. We must see them as instruments of growth. All things can be for our good if we but let them. This life is the time to prepare to live again with our Heavenly Father, to grow in spirit and character and strength to meet the challenges and tremendous responsibilities of the Celestial kingdom. We must be ever thankful for the trials that come in our lives because of the new experiences they bring, and the strength, understanding and growth that they afford us, that will help us to be better prepared to fulfill our responsibilities in the Celestial Kingdom."

As I sat there contemplating these truths that I had just been given, some more thoughts began to form in my mind that I felt Si would need to know. I quickly turned the page over and recorded what came into my mind. "This time of your life will be exciting and challenging as new experiences come to you. Remember, Si, that none of the talents that you have developed are lost — they are just temporarily put aside while you develop others."

A few days later, Si was going through a terrible time with shortness of breath and I shared with him these beautiful truths that had been given to me through the Holy Ghost, and they comforted him. I am grateful that I recorded them exactly as they were given so that they could bring comfort to him in his times of struggle.

Each day as I left the house to go to be with Si, I would have family prayer with my other children. We would take turns saying the prayer.

As each child prayed, they asked Heavenly Father to heal Si. I felt that Si's accident had a special purpose and that he would not be healed immediately. I felt that we not only needed to pray for this healing to occur, but we needed to ask Heavenly Father to help Si be strong and courageous, and to be able to handle this trial, that had come into his life, in a way that would be an influence for good in the lives of other people. These prayers were certainly heard and answered because Si was able to deal with whatever came to him with great faith and courage. Never once, in all that he went through, did he ever rail against his accident or the resulting trials. He just accepted them as Heavenly Father's will and tried to do the best that he could with what he had.

A couple of weeks after Si's accident happened, I got the feeling that maybe he thought that he was going to get better soon and so I asked him, "Si, what would you do if you could never walk or run again or play volleyball or draw or play the piano?" He thought for a moment and then he said, "Mom, I did those things the best I could do them when I could do them and now I'll do something else."

Si couldn't change his situation but he could certainly choose how he reacted toward it. He received his Patriarchal Blessing shortly after his accident happened. His blessing actually told him very little other than one great promise — that he would come to know his Heavenly Father's will for him. Through his great faith in the power of the Priesthood, he asked for and received many blessings of healing and comfort, and it was through these blessings that he came to understand, little by little, what his mission on earth was.

3
THE ICU

Si spent five months in the Respiratory Intensive Care Unit of the University Hospital. During that time, he went through many difficult trials, but also had some wonderful experiences.

The first month was spent in an isolation room that was separate from the rest of the ICU by windows and a door. One day they decided he needed to be moved out into the main room of the ICU. At that time Si was on a large Bennett respirator and attached to it were some bellows that moved up and down every time it breathed for him. The nursing staff told us that if the bellows didn't move, not to worry because sometimes they got stuck, but if the respirator wasn't working the alarm would go off.

When they moved him to his new location in the ICU, they forgot to plug in the alarm. That evening Si's Dad was there with him as usual, to brush his teeth for him and get him settled for the night. Frank was sitting beside Si reading, waiting for him to drop off to sleep. Suddenly the bellows on his respirator stopped moving. The alarm didn't go off so Frank assumed they were just stuck. He looked at Si who seemed to be sleeping peacefully. Frank just went on reading. What happened next is best told in Si's own words.

"I woke up because I wasn't getting any air. At that time, I couldn't make any sound so I could only wait to die — talk about a helpless feeling! Everything went black and then I was floating over my hospital bed. I saw Dad notice that I was blue so he called to the nurse that something was wrong with me. I saw Dad knock over a cup with a pencil in it in his haste to get help. I saw the doctors and nurses rush over and start working on me. Then I was back in my body with all the staff asking me if I was all right. I told Dad what I had seen while

my spirit was out of my body and he was speechless. I wonder what I would have seen if I had looked around. It didn't even occur to me to look around because I had been paralyzed for about a month and I couldn't turn my own head. Perhaps I would have seen the light at the end of a tunnel that so many people have described, but I didn't think to look. This experience showed me for certain that there is life after this one. Since then I have tried to keep an eternal outlook on things and that has helped me over the rough times in my life. I think it can help us all to get by a lot better in this life and make it easier to prepare for the life ahead. But I still wonder what I would have seen if I had looked around."

About a month after Si was moved into the main room of the ICU they did a tracheotomy on him so that he did not have to have a tube from the respirator in his mouth. This made it so much easier for me to communicate with him. I learned to read his lips quite easily and often felt as if I was actually hearing him speak.

The ICU had a rule that only family could visit. Si had many friends who were concerned about him and wanted to continue their friendship and association with him while he was in the intensive care unit. Since friends were not allowed to visit, whenever they would come to the unit and knock on the door to be admitted, they would say they were Si's brother or sister. After a few days of this, one of the nurses came up to me and said, "How many children do you have?!" Not knowing that Si's friends were doing this, I answered, "Six". And so their little trick was revealed. But because Si had to stay in the ICU for an extended period of time, the nursing staff realized that he needed the companionship of his friends. They bent the rules and allowed his friends to visit.

Some of his friends had a very hard time when they came into the ICU. Most of them got a little woozy and nearly fainted. One of them only got partway to Si's bed and had to leave. I found him sitting on the floor outside of the ICU door, looking very pale. One day Si's really good friend, Gisela, was visiting and all of a sudden she began to lean on me. I looked at her and knew she was about to faint so I carefully sat her down on the floor. I doubt if these dear young people will ever realize how much it meant to Si that they continued to visit and support him although it was difficult for them.

Another rule that the ICU had was that I was only able to visit 10 minutes out of every hour. The rest of the time I spent sitting in the ICU waiting room enduring the second hand smoke. Finally, I got the courage to talk with Dr. King (Si's Respiratory Doctor) about this. I told him that I wanted to be with Si every minute that I was allowed to be there because I felt he needed the emotional support that I could give him. I asked him if he would allow me to spend more time with Si. He agreed, and although some of the nurses were quite upset with this change in their rules, they reluctantly allowed me to come in and stay. I am very grateful for this because I was able to assist them in some of Si's treatments and learned how to do them. Thankfully I was able to spend many hours every day with Si because my mom was with my other children at home, and the Relief Society brought suppers to our family for over a month after the accident.

One of the nurses, however, was so upset by the rule-bending that she was mean to us. One day Si was really dehydrated due to a bad lung infection and was not able to take any fluids by mouth. His skin was hot and dry and he kept mouthing "water, water". The nurse, who was not happy that I was allowed to spend so much time in the ICU, came over to Si and said, "Si, you can't have any water so stop asking for it!" I asked if there was something they could give him, like ice, to take away the thirst that he was experiencing. She finally said, "Okay, Si, I'm going to give you some dye to swallow and if it comes out of your trachea hole, I know you can't swallow properly and I can't give you any water." I asked her to please not do that because I was afraid it might taste bad and I didn't want him to suffer any more than he already was. She just glared at me and told Si to open his mouth. He opened it and she put a glass vial filled with the dye into his mouth. Because Si was delirious from his fever, he bit down on the vial and it broke in his mouth. I panicked because I thought he would swallow the glass. I started to cry, and one of the other nurses told me that I should leave. They removed the glass from his mouth and then started giving him fluids intravenously to take away his dehydration. They ran the fluids into him so quickly that he began to bloat up. When they finally allowed me to come back into the ICU, he was swelled up like a balloon.

While I was in the waiting room, I called President Bob Patterson (a counsellor in our Stake Presidency) and asked him if he would come and give Si a blessing. He used to be our Bishop and had become a very dear and close friend. After his arrival, he gave Si a most beautiful blessing. He told him many comforting things but what I remember most was this one statement. He told Si that, through his influence, many people who did not know Heavenly Father or Jesus would come to know them. These were inspired words and this blessing certainly did come to pass!

After President Patterson left, a psychologist come in to evaluate Si's mental stability because he had bitten down on the glass vial. They would not allow me in the ICU while this was taking place. She asked Si where he lived and he did not hear her question. He asked her to repeat it. She couldn't read Si's lips so she asked him to spell the main word in the sentence that he was saying. He began to spell the word 'question'. She thought he was spelling "queen" and that this was his answer to where he lived. She called me in and told me that Si thought he lived in Queen. I asked Si what he was trying to say. He said, "I didn't hear her question, so I was spelling the word 'question' so that she would repeat it for me." I told her this and she concluded there was nothing wrong with Si's brain.

It wasn't until after Si's death, as I contemplated and marvelled at the things that he had gone through, that I fully appreciated his great strength and the courage he displayed. He couldn't even move his head and yet, through his indescribable suffering, he accepted it all.

Before Si was in the ICU I thought that it would be the quietest place in the hospital but, believe me, it wasn't! In fact, it was probably the busiest and noisiest place to be, aside from the ER. Because the patients required constant care around the clock, all the lights were never turned off and there was never a moment of peace and quiet.

One day, Corinne, one of Si's favourite nurses in the ICU, stopped me as I was leaving the ICU and asked if she could speak to me. We went into a little room that the doctors used to consult and comfort family members of patients in the ICU, and she told me that several of the nurses had a wager going on about how long it would take Si to break — to actually lose his sanity. My first reaction was to laugh and say, "That's not going to happen". I was shocked that the nursing staff would do something like that, but I appreciated her telling me because, when I shared that with Si, it made him more determined to be strong and to prove them wrong.

I am so grateful for the example of a good Latter-day Saint young man that Si was to the staff. Apparently, before Si came to the ICU, the language the nurses used was not very good. One day I had the opportunity to look at Si's chart and it read, 'Si is a religious boy and is offended by bad language so please watch what you say.'

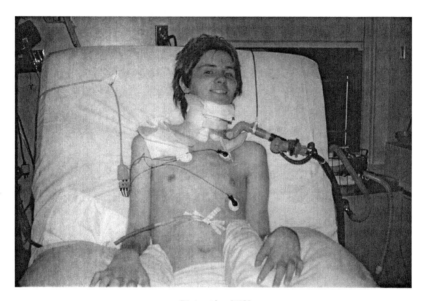

Si in the ICU

The only thing I could feel of my body was my head. One day my head didn't feel comfortable no matter what anyone did for me. My mom turned my head back and forth by inches and no matter where she placed it, it didn't feel right. Mom asked me how I could stand a big thing like having a broken neck and being totally paralyzed and not complain about it, but having my head not exactly right bothered me almost to the point that I couldn't stand it. I thought about that for a moment and then I said, "Well, Mom, it's like this. You know when you're walking outside in your bare feet and you step on a big rock, it doesn't really hurt. But if you step on a pebble, it almost kills you. Well, that's how it is with my head."

It was two weeks before my 17th birthday and it seemed there was no apparent means for my recovery. It looked like I would be spending my birthday in the hospital. That would be a very different kind of birthday and I wondered what it would be like.

When the day came, April 12, 1975, my Mom came up early to be with me all day. Since she always did this, I didn't think anything of it. When my mom suggested that we go down to the hospital lounge, I still didn't think anything of it because we had done that before. When we got to the lounge, it was full to overflowing with my friends. As we opened the door, they shouted, "Surprise!" I found out later that there were people lined up all the way down the hall, waiting to wish me a Happy Birthday. What a wonderful surprise this was for me! I was hardly expecting to be alive after the first month in the ICU, and now a surprise birthday party! People that knew me, knew that I liked music so many of them brought me tapes of my favourite music. One of my friends phoned CHED radio station and the crew there sang Happy Birthday to me over the radio. This was a super gift to me and one of the things that gave me strength during the difficult months that followed in the ICU.

For the birthday of each of my children, I would write a letter to them, expressing my love for them. The following is the letter I wrote to Si for his 17th Birthday.

April 12, 1975

My dear Si,

As I look out my window this morning at the beautiful day before me — my mind goes back to a similar spring day 17 years ago — for it was on such a day as this that you were born and Dr. Dorman placed you — my first precious little baby in my arms. I shall never forget the wonder, and love, and thankfulness that filled my heart that day. These beautiful feelings have increased each year as I have watched you grow and develop into a fine young man.

I have been sitting here for about an hour, lost in memories of the past 17 years I wish that I could share them all with you

2

today but I would like to
express in this letter my thoughts
& feelings of the past 6 weeks
of your life.

How very thankful I am
for the miracle of your life.
I feel, without any doubt, that
your life was spared for a very
special purpose and that dear
Heavenly Father will bless you
and give you the power both
physically & spiritually to fulfill
this purpose.

Some very spiritual things have
happened in our lives since your
accident Sr, and I shall always
be grateful to my Heavenly Father
for them. I would not trade
the precious moments that we
have spent together for anything
in the world.

3

Thank you for your beautiful
spirit and the courage & faith
that you have shown. You are
and have been a wonderful
example to us all.

There is a scripture that my
Grandma Schmidt used to quote
to me whenever I was with her.
It was her favorite and helped
her through the many trials of
her life. It has really helped me
too. I would like to share it
with you today & hope that it
will be a guide and an inspiration
to you also.

"Trust in the Lord with all
thine heart, and lean not unto
thine own understanding. In all
thy ways acknowledge him and
He will direct thy paths."

I know that you are one

of our Heavenly Fathers most precious spirits. I am eternally grateful that my Heavenly Father has given me the wonderful privilege of being your mother.

May you be blessed beyond measure in the coming years is my prayer for you.

Your loving mother

Anita

I suffered severe shortness of breath for most of the time that I was in the ICU. Having the lights on for 22 hours every day was very hard also. Just as I would get to sleep, someone would wake me up and tell me it was time to turn me or wash me or have my catheter irrigated or changed, or it was time for an x-ray or time for an installation (washing my lungs out with saline), etc., etc., etc. These treatments would take place during the day and night and so I got very little sleep. I almost felt like they were killing me with the care they were required to give me.

One of the worst things I experienced in the ICU was when the respiratory technicians tried to adjust my breathing. They put me on a rocking bed and at first anytime they turned it on and it would go up, I would pass out. After a while I got used to it. Then they decided that it would help if they synchronized the rocking bed movement with some things called phrenic pacers. I had an operation in which they isolated my phrenic nerves and implanted pacers around the nerve just below my collarbone. They were supposed to control my diaphragm *and help me breathe but, when they were turned on, they jerked me like I had a bad case of the hiccups. Mom and a technician named Al tried to synchronize the rocking bed with the pacers, and counted the respirations for many hours day after day for about a month, but to no avail. The only thing that came from that was they found out how long it would take for me to pass out, and I got two big sores on my chin from the neck brace. I know the Lord helped me and kept me from going crazy.*

This was a hard thing for Si to experience and a very difficult thing for me to watch him go through.

Si was in Grade 11 at Harry Ainlay High School when his accident happened. He had left his core subjects for his last semester, so he had a very heavy load. The Edmonton School Board sent tutors to the ICU to help Si continue his education. It was really slow going, however, because Si was sick with infections so much of the time and was often not well enough to be taught.

Finally the day came for me to move from the ICU. Although I didn't like it in the ICU one bit, it had been home for me for the past five months and I was scared to leave it. I felt secure there because I had someone with me 24 hours a day. Nevertheless I finally got over my fear of leaving.

My mom didn't want to send me to live in an institution. She thought she would be able to care for me at home but Dr. King, the head respiratory doctor, talked to her about the difficulty of undertaking such a task. He told her about a place called the Aberhart hospital and asked her to go with him to visit the patients there.

The first floor of the Aberhart hospital was the home of people who contracted polio during the 1950's epidemics, and also housed patients with respiratory problems.

I did go with Dr. King to visit the Aberhart Hospital and the first person he introduced me to was a polio patient named Gary MacPherson. I was very impressed with Gary. In spite of his great handicap, he was a very cheerful and positive person and I felt that he would be a great influence for good in Si's life.

The decision was made and, at the end of July 1975, Si was moved from the ICU to the Aberhart Hospital.

4

THE ABERHART HOSPITAL

Si had his own room in the Aberhart. It was right across from the nurse's station at the end of the long hall leading into the ground floor of the hospital. I felt comforted knowing he was so near to the nurse's station.

We fixed his room up to make it seem like home to him. Frank bought him really good stereo equipment and a TV that sat on a table over his bed. He had over a hundred LPs of all his favourite recording artists. Music was a very important part of Si's life. I put pictures up on his walls and tried to make it as homey as possible.

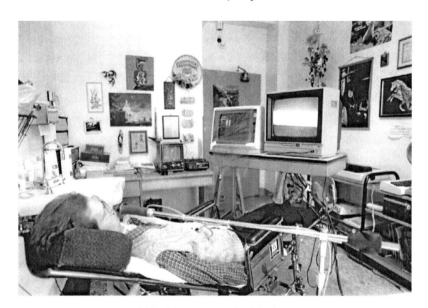

Si in his room at the Aberhart

The nursing staff were so kind to Si, and the orderlies became good friends to him. They would spend as much time as they could in his room listening to music with him. In fact, I think they did his care extra slowly because they enjoyed visiting with him. They would shut Si's door and when a nurse would knock to see what they were doing, they would say, "Don't come in yet. Si is not decent!" I'm sure the nurses knew what was going on but they never squealed on them. Unfortunately, that all changed a few years later with the cutback in nursing care that was experienced in all the hospitals.

A few weeks after Si moved to the Aberhart, we got word that the Mormon Tabernacle Choir was coming to Edmonton to perform at the Northland Coliseum. I really wanted to take Si to it but we didn't have a van, and the Aberhart van was not available.

We heard that President Nathan E. Tanner (a counsellor in the First Presidency of our church) was coming with the choir, so I phoned President Wilde, our Stake President, to see if he would ask President Tanner to visit Si and perhaps give him a blessing. President Wilde said he would see what he could do. He phoned back a few days later and said he thought there would be enough time for a visit before the concert. We were overjoyed! But then, their plane was delayed and they arrived in Edmonton behind schedule. President Wilde phoned again and said he didn't think there would be time. We were disappointed but we didn't give up hope. Imagine our great joy and delight when President Tanner and President Wilde walked into Si's room late that afternoon. Our prayers had been heard and answered.

President Tanner walked to the end of Si's bed and stood there looking at him. Then he said, "You are a very fine looking young man Si!" He then asked Si some questions and was able to read Si's lips very well. They visited for a few minutes and then President Tanner said, "Would you like a blessing Si?" I thought my heart would burst! Si of course said yes. President Tanner laid his hands on Si's head and gave him a most beautiful blessing. Among other things, he said that Si would be healed in our Heavenly Father's time. He told Si that his days on earth were set before he came to earth and they would not be numbered a day less. It was truly a blessing of comfort and brought peace to our hearts.

A prophet of God had visited Si and blessed him!

I spent many hours with Si each day reading to him, writing in his journal for him, and doing other things that he could not do for himself. I learned how to care for him as I watched the treatments he received from his respiratory therapists, physiotherapists, orderlies and nursing staff. I very much desired to have Si at home with our family and I knew that this would not happen until I was able to do all the things that needed to be done for him, so I was very grateful that they allowed me to learn from them.

Si's Dad, Frank, came up every evening to get Si ready for bed and to make sure he was comfortable for the night. I really appreciated the time he so willingly gave to him.

Si had many wonderful friends that visited him while he was in the Aberhart. Three of these friends, Gisela Walthers, Scott Bateman and Scott Duncan came to the hospital or to our home to spend time with him every Sunday evening for many years. They all learned to read Si's lips, and their time together as friends was so precious and important to him. They truly kept the covenant they had made when they were baptized, to 'comfort those who stand in need of comfort'. I know that they will be eternally blessed for the love and companionship they so unselfishly gave to Si.

Many people gave of their time to tutor Si in his school work. They did this by using correspondence courses. He took Math 20, Chemistry 20 and English 20, and passed all these courses with very good marks, thanks to the consistent and patient tutelage of these wonderful, caring people.

Jeannie Takahahashi — Si's English tutor, champion, and friend.

Although the members of our family tried to spend as many hours with Si as we could possibly manage, he still had times when he was alone with only his thoughts. I think it was during these times of quite reflection and prayer that he received the strength to face the life that he had been given. The anonymous poem "Silence" that I found in Mark Buchannan's book "Hidden in Plain Sight" describes, for me, how Si was able to hold on and not rail against his paralysis.

SILENCE

If you stand very still in the heart of a wood,
You will hear many wonderful things.
The snap of a twig, the wind in the trees,
And the whir of invisible wings.

If you stand very still in the turmoil of life,
And wait for the voice from within,
You'll be led down the quiet ways of wisdom and peace,
In a mad world of chaos and din.

If you stand very still, and hold onto our faith,
You'll receive all the help that you ask.
You will draw from the silence those things that you need,
Hope, courage and strength for the task.

A quiet moment.

Si was very careful what he allowed into his environment. He only listened to uplifting music and TV programs. One of his good friends painted a picture of the Saviour for Si that we hung on his wall over his stereo equipment. This picture helped Si remember to only listen to and watch those things that his Saviour would approve of.

Si had a wonderful sense of humour and a very teasing nature that was not diminished by his accident. He loved to play practical jokes on people. This art was used most often and repeatedly on me, his mother. He was really the king of one-liners. One day he was having a good time teasing me and I said to him, "Si, you are so weird you couldn't possibly be my son. You must have been adopted! But on second thought you look too much like your Dad to have been adopted." Without even blinking an eye Si said, "Well Mom, perhaps he was adopted too!" Another day I came into his room and he was listening to music. When I entered the room he asked me to turn the sound up because he couldn't hear it very well. I turned the sound up and he asked me to turn it up some more. It was still quite soft so I turned it as high as it would go. All of a sudden bells started to ring very loudly! It scared me so badly I nearly jumped out of my shoes. I looked over at Si and he was laughing his head off. He tried to tell me that that was the first time he had listened to that record, but I didn't believe him! Si had struck again!

5
HOME AT LAST

Finally the day came when I felt I could take Si home to spend the night. We hadn't purchased a van to transport him in, as yet, so a close friend, Bill Davis, brought Si home in his van.

A young man named Jamie Janes, who had spent a little time in the next room to Si at the Aberhart, had passed away, and his mother, at Jamie's request, had given Si his hospital bed and table. How very grateful we were for this thoughtful and needed gift.

We put the bed in the family room of our home that was next to the kitchen, so that Si would be where members of the family were, at all times. Because he couldn't breathe on his own we couldn't leave him alone for a minute.

Si was so happy to finally be able to be at home again, even if it was just for the night, and we were delighted to have him with us.

We had a wonderful evening and then it was time to get Si ready for bed. I undressed him, did his installation (washed his lungs out with normal saline), gave him his meds, brushed his teeth and settled him down for the night. I put a foam mattress on the floor beside his bed for me to sleep on.

The kids were all in bed. I lay down on my mattress and was just drifting off to sleep when I sat up with a start. I suddenly realized that Si did not have an alarm on his respirator and no alarm by his chin to alert me if he needed anything or if some hose came apart and he wasn't breathing. I was very tired and knew that I could never stay awake and alert all night, but I didn't dare go to sleep in case something came apart and he didn't get any air. I felt so alone and helpless and wondered why I had ever thought that I could bring him home and take care of him by myself. I lay back on my pillow and cried softly in fear and frustration. As I lay there wondering what I was going to do, a scripture that my Grandma Schneidt had recited to me over and over again throughout my life, came into my mind. ....."Trust in the Lord with all thine heart, and lean not unto thine own understanding. In all thy ways acknowledge Him, and He will direct thy paths." Proverbs 3:5

As the truth of this wonderful scripture entered my mind, I realized that all I had to do was trust in my Heavenly Father and He would not let me do anything that would put Si's life in jeopardy. Si was in His hands, not mine. He had a special mission for Si to accomplish here on the earth and He would watch over him and protect him and wake me if Si needed me.

An overwhelming feeling of peace came over me and I cried with relief and joy. How very grateful I am for my wonderful Grandma who taught me this beautiful scripture. It was as if she knew I would someday need to know it and to live by it.

I went to sleep and exactly two hours later I awoke to turn Si. I did that throughout that night and every night that I cared for him when he was at home. It was almost as if an angel gently woke me every two hours so that I could turn my son throughout the night. I am convinced that that is exactly what happened and I am grateful for the spiritual help that I received.

Si finally received a respirator that had a built-in alarm that sounded if a hose came disconnected or if his volumes decreased. What a great blessing this was for me as I continued to bring Si home on the weekends and for holidays, when my other children were home to help me.

We finally purchased a used Dodge maxi van so that we were able to bring Si home whenever we wanted to without having to rely on the availability of the hospital van or DATS (Disabled Adult Transportation System). What a great blessing that was to us.

It was not equipped with a lift so we got Si into it using ramps. This was quite difficult because of the heaviness of the wheel chair, the respirator, and the batteries that ran the respirator, that were all on the back of the chair. But with me pushing and one of my children pulling we were able to manage.

A few months later, the Primary children of our Stake began saving their pennies and donating them to help purchase a hydraulic lift for Si's van. It didn't take them very long until they had given enough money and the lift was purchased and installed. I shall always be grateful for the unselfish service these dear children gave. We were now able to get Si in and out of the van very easily.

Although Si's brother, David, was only 14 years old when Si had his accident, he became quite expert at keeping Si's equipment running properly. He also was my chief chauffeur whenever we took Si out of the hospital.

My oldest daughter, Lori, was such a great help to me, also. I don't know what I would have done without her. She was 15 when Si had his accident and, although she had always been a big help to me as my oldest daughter, she became like my right arm. She would take the bus from school to the Aberhart to be with Si so I could go home and get supper for the family and be with my younger children, or she would go home and make supper and take care of the family for me if Si was not well and needed me to be with him. Both David and Lori grew up very quickly, as a result of this accident, and rarely exhibited any of the behaviours or attitudes that are so common to teenagers. As my other children got older, they too learned how to care for Si, and became such wonderful helpers to me.

Si's youngest brother, Benjie, who was eight years old when the accident happened, was always very fearful when we brought Si home. He was so afraid that something would happen to Si. I didn't realize the extent of his fear until I began noticing that every time we decided to bring Si home, Ben would ask if he could sleep over at a friend's house. I always tried to have at least one of the children at home with me whenever Si was there — in case of an emergency. One evening, all of my older children were going out so I asked Ben if he could stay home with me. I knew he really didn't want to but he said yes.

All went smoothly for a few hours. I was busy getting supper and Benjie was watching TV. Si was having a little nap — or so I thought. When I went to turn him I noticed that his face was very pale and his lips were quite blue. I tried to wake him but he didn't respond. I then noticed that the cap of his tracheostomy appliance that we suctioned through was not on properly and he was not getting all the air he needed. He was only getting enough to keep his alarm from going off. I quickly grabbed his bagger and began to give him air. I asked Benjie to please call for an ambulance. Benjie ran to the phone. He told me later that he felt like he was going to faint but prayed to Heavenly Father for strength so he could do what I had asked him to do. He dialed 911 and very calmly told the dispatcher to send an ambulance to 5819 – 114 A St. because his brother was dying. He said that he was shaking so badly he could hardly dial the number, but he did what was required of him. By the time the ambulance arrived, we had Si back and everything was alright.

I was so grateful for this little son of mine, for his faith in his Heavenly Father and the strength he received from Him to help in an emergency. Interestingly, after that incident, he wasn't afraid to stay at home when Si was there over night.

6

SI'S FIRST HOLIDAY

In the summer of 1976, we decided to take Si on his first holiday after his accident. He wanted to go to southern Alberta to visit his relatives. The staff of the Aberhart filled the whole back of our van with all of the supplies that Si would need for a week's holiday. I could not believe the amount of equipment that was needed to care for him. Frank's mother, Grandma Ostby, was visiting so she traveled down with us. David drove and we took Benjie, Barbie, Leigh Ann, Sandy (our dog), Benjie's gerbil (Snoopy) and, of course, Si. Lori did not go with us because she had a job working in her Dad's dental office.

Before we left Edmonton, we stopped at Darrel Hudson's house and asked him to offer a prayer for our safety. (Darrel was one of our dearest and closest church friends) All went well until we got to Calgary. It was rush- hour time and we were on MacLeod Trail, right in front of Chinook Shopping Center, when the battery on the van went dead. We had an extra battery with us in case the battery that ran Si's respirator went dead, so in the middle of rush- hour traffic, David changed the battery, and we proceeded on our way. We got to my sister and brother-in-law's house in Raymond without further incident. But the next day, the van's battery was dead again. We boosted it and took the van to a mechanic. He said that we needed a new alternator. He put one in and we didn't have any further trouble on that trip.

Si had a wonderful time visiting with his many relatives. My sister, Eltie, had a hospital bed that she set up in her living room for Si so that he was very comfortable. I slept on a couch beside his bed.

7

AN OUT-OF BODY EXPERIENCE

In September of 1976, we felt that Si could possibly attend school each day to take his Math 20 course that he hadn't completed before his accident. I registered him in that class at Harry Ainlay High School.

He attended the first day of school and enjoyed seeing his friends again and being able to be with them.

When we got back to the hospital after his class, I helped the orderly lift him into bed and then I left to go home to pick up Lori to stay with him while I got supper ready. At this time we tried to have someone with Si constantly. I dropped Lori off at the hospital and returned home. As I walked in the door, the phone was ringing. It was Lori and she said that something bad had happened to Si and that I should come back quickly. I returned to the hospital immediately. As I walked up the hallway, Lori came to meet me. She said that when she got there Si's door was closed and several nurses and doctors were in with him. I rushed into Si's room and his bed was surrounded by hospital staff. He looked very grey and I thought he was dead. They asked me to leave.

What had happened was, after I left to go get Lori, Si needed suctioning and so he rang for the nurse. She came and suctioned him but forgot to put the elastic over the cap on his tracheostomy tube to hold it on. It often popped off without the elastic. As she finished suctioning him, someone else's bell rang and she went out in a hurry and also forgot to put Si's alarm switch beside his chin. She told him she would be right back. A few minutes later, the cap on Si's tracheostomy tube popped off and he had no way to call for help. He clicked several times but no one came. When the nurse finally came back, 20 minutes had passed, and, because Si was not receiving any air for most of that time, he had gone under. She called for help and began bagging him. His heart had stopped. The doctors began attempting to get it started again. Finally they got it going but he had hardly any blood pressure.

Lori and I ran to call Brother Hudson, our Home Teacher, and then we went into a small room and said a most fervent prayer. Brother Hudson came and we sat outside Si's room together. After a half an hour had passed, I felt that I should tell them to stop trying to revive him and just let him go, but every time I tried to get up off my chair, I could not get up. I told Brother Hudson what I wanted to do but that I could not get up. He said that I probably wasn't supposed to and that we should wait a little longer.

Quite a few more minutes passed and then a doctor came out of Si's room and said, "We have Si's heart started but he is in a deep coma and I am afraid that, if he does wake up, he will be in a vegetative state because he did not have any air for such a long time." The doctor told us that he had called an ambulance to take Si to the ICU in the University Hospital. I asked him if we could see Si before the ambulance came and he said yes. We went in and Brother Hudson gave Si a Priesthood blessing. In the blessing all he said was, "We pray, Father, that Thy will be done." The ambulance came and I went with Si to the University Hospital. I stayed with him all night and talked to him in case he could hear me, so that he wouldn't be frightened. He did open his eyes but they never focused on me and he never blinked.

About noon, I decided to go home and get freshened up. When I got there, I phoned Bob Cowan, Si's favorite orderly, to tell him what had happened because he had not been working at the time. He said, "Get back up to the hospital right away and I'll meet you there." He lived in Sherwood Park (a town east of Edmonton) and he got there at the same time I did, so he must have almost flown the whole way.

We got to the door of the ICU where Si was and rang the bell to be admitted. Only family members were allowed in the ICU so when the nurse came to the door, Bob said, "Hi, I'm Si's brother" so she let him in with me. He walked over to Si's bed and said, "Hi Si, you old guy. What the heck are you doing in here?" Si blinked his eyes and said, "Hi Bob". A miracle had occurred! Si was back! I phoned the Aberhart and told them and the nurses ran up and down the hall yelling, "Si's back, Si's back!"

When I talked to the doctor later, he said, "A greater power than anything we could do or have done has brought Si back."

That afternoon we took Si back to the Aberhart.

During the time that Si's heart had stopped, he actually visited the Spirit World and told me some wonderful things that he had seen.

The next day, early in the morning, Si's nurse called me and said that something was not right with him — that he had stopped talking. (Si couldn't talk out loud so we had to read his lips, but he had stopped moving his lips.) I went right up to the hospital to see what was wrong. I asked Si several questions, but he just looked at me and didn't answer. This went on for several days and then one morning, his nurse called again and said, "Come up. Si is talking again!" I hurried to the hospital and sure enough, Si was back to his old self again. I asked him why he hadn't answered us and he said, "I answered every one of your questions and you kept asking me the same things over and over." He had thought his lips were moving and that he was talking to us. We think that his tongue and lips must have become paralyzed too, so he couldn't feel that they were not moving. Perhaps this happened to him so that he couldn't talk about the wonderful things that he had experienced in the Spirit World because, after that, he wasn't able to remember them. Si suffered no further complications from this experience, and his brain was not damaged in the least.

A miracle had occurred!

8
ADVENTURES

I very rarely took Si out of the hospital by myself. This was an unwise thing to do because if anything went wrong I wouldn't be able to take care of him and drive at the same time. But one day I was visiting with Si and it was time to go home and take the kids to Primary (our church's children's organization). It was such a nice day out that I asked Si if he would like to go for a little drive. He readily accepted. I got him into the van and drove home. I left Si alone in the van while I ran into the house to get the kids. As I was leaving the house to go back out to the van, the phone rang and, because it was right by the front door and I could see Si in the van, I answered it. As I was talking on the phone, I noticed that Si was mouthing something so I hung up quickly and ran to the van. The alarm on his respirator was ringing. The battery that his respirator was running with had gone dead. I grabbed Si's bagger and tried to hitch it up to his hose but I couldn't get his hose apart to put the bagger on. I struggled with it for several minutes, and when I looked at Si his face was very pale and he had passed out. I finally was able to get his bagger attached and began bagging him. I bagged and bagged for what seemed like an eternity, all the time praying that he would come back. Finally the color began returning to his neck and face and he woke up. I was so relieved that I started to cry. Si noticed how emotional I was and said something very profound that was a great source of comfort to me. He said," Mom, as long as I am meant to be here and Heavenly Father wants me here, you will always be here in time and know what to do for me."

The orderlies at the Aberhart were so good to Si. Two of them, Bob Cowan and Bob Tomniak, were his favorites. They sometimes took Si to the shopping mall. They would sit on the couches in the middle of the mall aisles and let Si 'people watch'. Sometimes children or teen-agers would come up and ask what happened to Si. With a very straight face Bob would say, "Oh, he was on drugs really bad. You better not ever take drugs!" or he would say some other equally scary thing. Si said he had a really hard time not laughing, but he hoped it kept these young people from taking drugs.

One sunny summer afternoon some of the orderlies, who had the day off, decided to take Si to a lake where one of them had a cabin. They asked me to go with them. There was a boat there and everyone had a good time going for rides and water skiing. One of the orderlies asked Si if he would like to go for a ride in the boat. Si, of course, said yes because he was a real daredevil, but I did not feel very comfort-able about him going out in a boat. Besides, I didn't know how he was going to breathe while he was out in it. But to them it was very simple! One of them put a lawn chair in the boat for Si to lay on. One of them carried Si to the boat while I bagged him using a portable ventilator, and another one brought his respirator so we could hitch him up to it after he was settled in the boat. It all went so smoothly that I could hardly believe it. Si had a great time. The pure joy on his face, as he went around and around the lake, made it worth all the risks.

As I mentioned in the introduction, Si was a really good artist before his accident. One day we were informed that mouth-painting classes were being held in the city. I asked Si if he would like to go and learn how to mouth paint. He got really excited. I took him a few times until his health deteriorated again and he wasn't able to continue.

This was an interesting experience for Si and a rather frustrating experience for me. Si was not able to move his own head at all so all of the movement of the paint brush had to be done with his lips.

He decided to paint a landscape and he did a rather remarkable job in the few lessons he was able to attend. He painted the sky, some hills, the ground, and a tree. I was so proud of him and his desire to do his best at whatever he tried to do.

It was a frustrating experience for me, however, because, as he tried and tried to make the brush go where he wanted it to go, I just wanted to take it out of his mouth and do it for him. It was so hard for me to stand beside him and watch him struggle. My heart ached for him. But my heart also soared when I saw what his patience and perseverance produced.

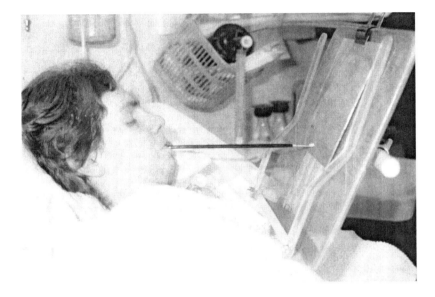

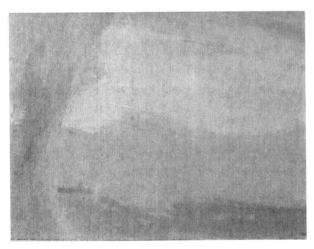

9
"HAPPINESS IS BEING MARRIED TO A DUTCHMAN"

The year 1978 brought some wonderful and unexpected changes in my life that also had a profound influence on Si's life.

It was a Sunday evening in early May and I had just brought Si back to the hospital from his weekend at home when Marinus Begieneman and his daughter Kathleen came up to visit him. I stayed and we had a very nice visit together.

Just before they left, Marinus asked if Si would like to go to a concert with him the following Thursday evening at the Museum Theatre. Of course this meant that I would also have to go along because Marinus did not know how to care for Si, and we needed to use our van to take Si there. Si was really excited to go, so we accepted the invitation.

Wednesday evening, as I was bringing Si home from an Institute class, the lift on his van stopped working so there was no way we would be able to take him to the concert the next evening. I phoned Marinus and told him what had happened, and he asked me if I would still like to go. Marinus had been divorced from his wife a few months before this, so I decided that this would be alright.

We went to the concert, which caused quite a stir among the members of our church that were there, but we pretended not to notice and had a very nice time. We went for milkshakes after and had a good time talking about our children and our lives. In the course of the conversation, Marinus mentioned that he was going down to the Cardston Temple the next afternoon and would be attending a wedding there on Saturday morning.

That Sunday was Mother's Day and I really wanted to spend it with my Mom who'd had a stroke, and was in the hospital in Cardston. I thought that perhaps Marinus wouldn't mind if I rode down with him. I asked Si if he would be alright if I left him for a couple of days. He assured me he would be fine, so I got on the phone and tried to find the Government Department that Marinus worked for to ask him if I could ride with him. I didn't know if he worked for the Provincial or the Federal Government, so I had to call almost every department in each before I finally located him. He seemed pleased that I had asked to accompany him. He picked me up in the afternoon and we were on our way. We decided to try to make it to the last evening session of the Temple, but we got to Cardston just as the session was starting so we were not able to go.

I asked Marinus where he was planning to stay for the night and he said he was going to go to a motel in Lethbridge. I invited him to come to my Dad's house in Welling, where I was staying, because there was plenty of room there. He accepted and spent the night there.

Before retiring, we made plans to go to a movie the next night, after I had spent the day with my Mom.

Marinus left early the next morning to attend the Temple wedding, and I went to Cardston with my Dad to visit my Mom.

Marinus picked me up there that evening, and we went into Lethbridge to a movie and to have dinner.

We had a nice time together.

The next morning was Mother's Day, so my Dad left early to be with my Mom. Marinus and I had decided to go to Sunday School in Welling and then leave for home. As I was getting ready, I noticed Marinus walking around outside in the barnyard and wondered what he was doing. He came in and called to me to come into the living room, so that he could talk to me. We sat down across the room from each other and he said, "I haven't slept at all the whole night because the Spirit has told me that I am to ask you to be my wife."

I looked at him and knew that was the right thing to do, so I said, "Yes that would be right". We hugged each other and he gave me a very tender kiss, and we went across the road to Sunday School.

Marinus' four daughters, Kathleen, Leslie, Renee and Monique, and all of my children were very excited about this wonderful event and could hardly wait for our marriage, so we could be one big happy family.

My daughter Lori was getting married in July so I asked Marinus if we could be married after her, so that I could concentrate on making her wedding a special event. We set August 12th for our wedding day and we were married that day in the Cardston Temple.

As I look back on this amazing event in my life, I can see so clearly how my Heavenly Father was over it all. He knew that my children had to go on with their own lives — Lori to get married, and David to go on his mission, and that I would be left without these two wonderful people to help me with Si. Heavenly Father knew that I couldn't do it all alone, so he sent a wonderful man into my life just when I needed someone the most. And what a blessing my Marinus has been to me and to my family.

Because of him, Si was able to do so many more things in his life that he would never have been able to do without the help, encouragement, and inspiration of his 'Dad B. (Happiness is being married to a DUTCHMAN.)

Si's family 1984. Back row left to right: Renee Begieneman, Barbara Peterson, Leslie Begieneman, Leigh Ann Peterson, David Peterson, Lori Peterson Eakett, Monique Begieneman, Kathleen Begieneman Carter, Benjie Peterson. Front row left to right: Marinus (Dad B.), Si Peterson, Anita (Mom B).

In the summer of 1978, before Marinus and I were married, he helped me take Si on another holiday to Southern Alberta. Marinus drove the van and David and Benjie followed us in our car. It was wonderful having a man along with us. He made us feel safer.

We had a wonderful time that week visiting with all of our relatives and then it was time to go home. We were a few miles out of Fort MacLeod in a terrible rain storm, when the alternator on the van stopped working again. Marinus managed to pull the van to the side of the road before it completely died.

We had Si's respirator plugged into the van's battery and also had the air conditioner running, so I guess it was just too much for the alternator to handle. When the van stopped, Si's respirator was supposed to switch over to the battery on his chair, but it was also dead. Si was not getting any air! I began to bag him while Marinus changed the battery on his chair with the extra one that we had brought along, but that battery was also dead!

Benjie and David stopped behind us and Marinus ran back to ask them to go into Fort McLeod and get an ambulance to come to take Si to the hospital. I continued to bag Si and as I was bagging him, the cuff, which is a small balloon surrounding the tracheostomy appliance in his throat, got a leak in it, so most of the air that I was giving him with the bagger, was not going into his lungs.

Finally an ambulance arrived, but unfortunately, they had sent a station wagon ambulance that proved to be quite difficult to get Si's wheelchair into. We were on the side of the road next to a very deep ditch. The ambulance driver and Marinus had to lift Si, in his wheelchair, off the ramp in the pouring rain and carry him to the ambulance. All the time they were doing this, I had to keep bagging him. Somehow we managed to get him into the ambulance and I went with him to the hospital. Marinus and the boys followed in the car.

Marinus called a tow truck and they towed the van to a repair shop and then Benjie and Marinus went on to Edmonton in the car because Marinus had to work the next day. David stayed with me and Si at the hospital.

As soon as we got Si settled in a room, I plugged his respirator in so I didn't have to continue bagging him, but because his cuff was leaking, I had to keep putting air into his cuff with a syringe, every few minutes.

I asked the nurse on duty if she could change Si's tracheostomy appliance, but she said that she could not do it, and we would have to wait until the charge nurse came in the morning. I had to continue putting air into Si's cuff every few minutes all through the night so that he would not die. I prayed so hard that I would be able to stay awake and alert to keep Si safe. There was another bed in the room, and David went to sleep on that.

The charge nurse came at 7:00 the next morning and I asked her if she would change Si's tracheostomy appliance. She agreed to do it, so I set everything up for her. She was just about to take Si's old tracheostomy appliance out when she asked, "Can Si breathe at all on his own?" I told her no, and she said that she did not feel comfortable doing this procedure in case she was not able to get the new trach back in. She felt that we should wait for the doctor to do it. I asked her what time the doctor would be there and she said that he usually came in around 1:00 p.m. I went back to putting air in Si's cuff every few minutes until the doctor finally arrived.

He came into the room and asked what the problem was. I told him that Si's tracheostomy appliance needed to be changed because the cuff was leaking and he said, "Oh, I think I can fix that." Normally Si's cuff requires 10 ccs of air but he proceeded to fill a syringe with 30 ccs of air which would have caused the cuff to rupture in Si's throat. Si had a look of terror on his face. I then realized that the doctor did not know what to do, so I said, "Please don't do that!" I then explained that I could change Si's trach if he would just stand by me with an intubation tray to intubate Si through his mouth if I was not able to get the trach appliance in again. He said he would do that, and got an intubation tray ready. I had never changed Si's trach before, but I had seen it done many times. I got everything ready. As I was putting on the sterile gloves, I realized my hands were shaking badly because I was so scared. I knew I had to do it though, so I went ahead and did the procedure as I had seen it done. It took less than a minute. After I had successfully inserted his new trach appliance, the doctor looked at me and said, "You can stop shaking now, Mom. You've done it!"

I am so grateful to Heavenly Father that He again heard my prayers and helped me to successfully do something that I had never done before. Another miracle!

David walked to the garage and picked up the van. We loaded Si in and went on our way home.

10
THE ULCER

We brought Si home for the weekend, as usual, on Saturday, February 17, 1979. For the past week or so, he had not been feeling really well. He had felt nauseated much of the time and always seemed to have a cold sweat on his face. We thought perhaps it was a flu bug because many of the people in the hospital had been sick with the flu. He didn't feel really well all weekend and seemed tired all the time. We took him to Church but he kept getting really dizzy and had to be tipped back, in his chair, almost constantly. Marinus was at home with a severe case of tonsillitis and I really missed having him with me. David helped me take Si back to the hospital.

About 8:00 a.m. Monday morning the phone rang and it was Sandy, the charge nurse at the hospital. She said that Si was not well and that I should come as soon as possible. I hurried to get dressed and rushed up to the hospital. Doctors were working on Si trying to get an IV started. He was hemorrhaging quite badly from his bowels and through his stomach tube hole. It was old black blood, so they figured he must have been bleeding internally for at least 48 hours. They weren't sure what was causing it, but they were extremely concerned. By the time the doctors got there that morning around 7:00, Si's blood pressure had dropped very low and his heart was barely beating. They were really worried because he needed a transfusion immediately and they were unable to start an IV. Although Si was in shock, he was still able to maintain his sense of humour and optimistic outlook. The doctors and nurses were very surprised at this. Finally, after an hour and a half of struggling, they were able to start two IV's, one in his left foot and one in his left arm. They did a cut down on his right ankle but were unable to start one there. That afternoon, the doctor started another one in his right arm. I stayed with him all day and evening, and he had no fresh bleeding at all.

I went up to Si early the next morning and stayed with him all day. Blood was still draining out of his stomach, but except for one little red clot, it was all old blood. The doctor took me into the empty room next to Si's room and told me that Si was in very serious condition. They still were not sure what was causing the bleeding, but if it was a duodenal ulcer it could bleed profusely at any time. He asked me how hard I wanted them to try to save Si's life, if something like this should happen. He seemed sorry that he had to ask me this. I quickly assured him that I felt that Si would someday be healed, and I wanted them to do everything possible to keep him alive. He was quite relieved when I said this. The night before, after Family Home Evening, Marinus and Darrel Hudson came up to the hospital and administered to Si. As Marinus sealed the anointing, he blessed Si that his life would be spared and he would recover. I felt so relieved and thankful for the power of the Priesthood and for these two wonderful men who held and honoured it and were worthy to give this blessing. I was still worried about Si, however, and what he might have to go through, but I felt a peaceful assurance that he would be all right.

Karen Redd, my visiting teaching companion, picked me up at the hospital about 7:00 p.m. Tuesday evening and we went Visiting Teaching. Marinus stayed with Si while I was gone. We had four ladies to visit so we didn't get back to the hospital until 9:00 p.m.

As I walked in the door, I saw Marinus coming down the hall and he looked very worried. He said that at about 8:00, Si had started to bleed fresh blood and they were going to take him to the ICU as soon as the ambulance arrived. Si had had some very bad experiences in the ICU, so he was quite upset about going, but after talking to him for a few minutes, he calmed down and again accepted what was happening to him, calmly and cheerfully. As we were moving him from the bed to the ambulance stretcher, both of his IV's became disconnected and blood ran all over Si and the bed. It was really a horrible mess. Two nurses, Mrs. Dickson and Sue Anne, rode with Si in the back of the ambulance and I rode in the front. Marinus went home to take care of the family.

I helped get Si settled in his bed in the ICU. They had a new ICU unit and it was so much bigger and nicer than the old one that Si was not unhappy about being there at all. He was put in a separate glassed-in-room and it even had an easy chair for me to sit in. They said they were going to tap an artery for his blood gases, so I was sent out to the waiting room. Frank came, and about 11:00 p.m. they let us back in to see Si. Instead of tapping an artery, they had started another IV in the main vein in his neck as the ones in his arms had stopped working. While doing this, they had punctured the upper part of his lung, which necessitated putting a tube in his plural cavity to drain off the blood and fluid. In spite of all this, Si was cheerful and calm as we visited with him. The courage and faith of this wonderful son was truly amazing to me. He was called to bear so very much and did it well. I will be forever grateful for the example he was to me.

On Wednesday, February 21st, they put Si under general anaesthetic and put a tube down his throat to look at his stomach. They found that his stomach tube had been pushed too far in and was in his duodenum. When they pulled it out, he bled so profusely that they were unable to see what was causing the bleeding.

I stayed with Si all day again and read to him. I felt so close to him and was so thankful that I could stay with him.

On Thursday, February 22nd, they looked into Si's stomach again and found that there was a huge clot in his duodenum. When they tried to move it, he hemorrhaged really badly so they just came out and left it. Si had been given blood transfusions steadily since he came into the ICU, but he seemed to be losing it as quickly as it went in. The doctors had given Si massive doses of a new drug that was supposed to heal duodenum ulcers. They decided to just wait and see if the medicine would help and he would not have to be operated on.

I went up to Si early the next morning and he seemed quite well all day. He was still bleeding but there was no fresh blood. I went out to the waiting room at 1:30 p.m. because no one was allowed in the ICU between 1:30 and 3:00. Lori came about 2:30 and we went to get a sandwich. When we came back at 3:00, one of the people sitting in the waiting room said that the ICU had called for me. I phoned in and they said that I couldn't go in because the doctors were busy with Si. I waited a few minutes and called again but they said that Si had started to bleed very badly, and he was being rushed to the operating room. I begged them to let me in to see him for a minute but they said that I would be in the way. Lori and I went immediately into an empty room and offered a fervent prayer for Si and for the doctors who would be operating on him. We then went back to the door of the ICU. A doctor came out and I asked him if we could please see Si for just a minute, and he said we could but hoped we wouldn't get upset because blood had spilled all over and the room was a terrible mess. I couldn't have cared less about the room. I just wanted to see my Si. They were just wheeling him out when we got in there, but I was able to see him and tell him how much I loved him. Lori and I tried to follow them down to the operating room, but by the time I signed the release forms, they were too far ahead of us. The nurse told us that it would be best if we waited in the ICU waiting room because they would receive word first. We went back to the waiting room and called Marinus, Frank, and Brian (Lori's husband). They all came and we waited together. I prayed so hard, throughout those long hours of waiting, that Si's life would be spared again. And again, I had that comforting, peaceful feeling come to me that our Heavenly Father was over the situation and whatever His will was concerning Si would be done and be best for all.

Finally, Dr. Turner, the surgeon, appeared and asked Frank and me to come with him. We went a short ways down the hall and then he told us that Si had come through the operation really well. He said that they would be bringing him up to the ICU soon, and that we would be able to see him. I cannot describe the joy and thankfulness that filled my heart at those words. Dr. Turner told us that they had found two large ulcers. One was growing into Si's liver and one was in his pancreas. They were able to successfully remove them, but also had to remove part of his stomach. He said that there was a marvelous new drug for ulcers now, and if Si was given this from then on, he probably would not get any more ulcers. How very grateful I was that our Heavenly Father had blessed the men of science with the knowledge and technical skills to help our Si through his trials.

Si recovered very quickly from this operation and was able to return to the Aberhart on Monday, February 26th.

Thursday, April 12, 1979 was Si's 21st birthday. We brought him home from the Aberhart and had a special supper and a little party for him. Brian and Lori came over and brought him a huge box of all kinds of candy. He really had fun 'pigging out' all the next week. Si stayed home with us all the Easter week and part of the next week because there was a lot of flu at the hospital and they were short of staff. We really enjoyed having him home with us, and I didn't even get too tired at all. The first two days were always the hardest, but then I got used to the routine of waking up every 2 hours to turn Si, and sometimes in between to suction him, and I was able to carry on quite well.

On Friday, May 11th, we had another frightening experience with Si. We brought him home from the hospital around suppertime. He ate a good supper and then watched TV until 11:00. I got him ready for bed and he settled down and went right to sleep. At about 1:00 a.m., his lungs began to fill with mucous, so I asked him if he would like to be suctioned. He didn't wake up when I spoke to him, so I thought that he must be really tired. I went ahead and suctioned him. It was then time to turn him, so I asked him if he would like to be turned. He still didn't respond, so I turned him. He didn't even open his eyes all the time I was doing this. I began to be concerned because he usually woke up very easily. David came in right then, and I told him that I couldn't wake Si up. He turned the light on over Si's bed. Si didn't even blink, but went right on sleeping. I became really alarmed then, and went up and woke Marinus. We did everything we could to wake Si up, but he would not respond. I phoned an ambulance and, while we were waiting for it to come, Marinus and David administered to Si. Marinus offered a beautiful blessing and commanded Si, through the Priesthood's power, to wake up and to be all right because he had a mission to fulfill here on the earth, and it was not time for him to leave this life.

The ambulance came and Marinus and I went with Si to the University Hospital. On the way there, Si opened his eyes, but he didn't seem to be able to focus them, and he was not able to talk. Saliva was drooling from his mouth.

We stayed in the emergency room at the hospital until about 4:00 a.m. During this time, Si tried to talk, but he couldn't seem to make his tongue work properly. No one there knew what to do for him, so we took him, by ambulance, to the Aberhart. The doctor said that he would order an EEG for Si the next day. After we got to the Aberhart, Marinus took a taxi home, and I stayed with Si until 10:00 the next morning.

Around 6:00 a.m., Si really woke up and was able to talk to me. He was very confused and couldn't remember anything that had happened and kept asking why he was back in the Aberhart instead of at home. By the time I left at 10:00 a.m., he was quiet and back to normal again. His EEG came back normal. I am grateful for the power of the Priesthood, because I know that he was made better through the blessing that was given him.

11

BLESSINGS AND TRIBULATIONS

On Sunday, March 16, 1980, we heard a program on CHED radio station called "Sunday at 9:00". Bob Layton, one of CHED's announcers, and a member of our Church, hosted the program. The subject of his program that day was Si's story.

Prior to this segment being aired, Bob interviewed Si, Si's brother David, Si's Institute class teacher Dale LeBaron, Si's doctor, and me, and then put it together in a ½ hour program. I was filled with a feeling of love and gratitude for Si's life and his example of faith and courage as I listened to this program. I was grateful that he had the opportunity to express his thoughts and testimony, and I was sure that it would strengthen all who heard it. The station had a policy to never air one of these segments more than once, but when Si's story was aired, the response was so overwhelming that they repeated it several times.

The opening of a new chapel, the Riverbend Stake Center, was to be held in November 1980. Bob Layton was asked to produce a slide presentation called "The Si Peterson Story" that would be presented during the week of the open house. Kent Richardson was asked to take the pictures to go along with the soundtrack that Bob had writen for the "Sunday at Nine" radio program about Si. An audio-visual package was created that told about how Si's accident had occurred and recounted some faith promoting incidents that Si had experienced during the 5 years since his accident happened. As Kent was planning on serving a mission, we asked him to live with us so that he could save money for his mission and also be able to more easily take the pictures that were needed for the slide show. He became another member of our family.

Si suffered very bad health in the weeks before the opening of the Stake Center, and we were very fearful that he might not be able to attend. But, through fasting and prayer and Priesthood blessings, miracles occurred, and he was made well again. The following are accounts of his suffering and his miraculous recovery.

One evening Si's Dad phoned me, while he was visiting with Si, and said that Si was not feeling very well and seemed really drowsy. We decided that it might be a build-up of all the meds he was receiving. It really worried me because he acted like that just before he went into that deep sleep. I phoned Sandy Baker, the charge nurse, the next morning, and told her my concerns. She said that they would do tolerance tests for the Dilantin and Dantrium that he was given to control his spasms. She also told me that Si had a urinary tract infection and a lung infection and that they had given him a very large dose of antibiotic and would give him another one that evening. They were hoping that this would stop the infections and he would not have to go on IV's.

When I visited Si that day, he was lying in his room with all the drapes pulled and was listening to music. His eyes were really puffy, and he was very tired. His tongue was quite swollen, and he was unable to eat anything by his mouth.

About 3:00 a.m. the next morning the phone rang and it was the hospital. Si was not feeling well and he wanted me to come. I quickly dressed and was at the hospital in a few minutes. His arms were hurting really badly so I exercised them for him and then sat by him and stroked his hair until he felt sleepy. I was prepared to stay with him the whole night, but he said that he would be all right and that I could go home.

I phoned the hospital at 8:00 a.m. and found out that Dr. Brown would be coming for rounds that morning. I wanted to talk to him so I left for the hospital. Si seemed a little more alert although his eyes were still quite swollen and his face was still puffy. His abdomen had been quite distended the night before so Malcolm, the orderly, was attempting a bowel routine on him.

They did several tests on Si to determine the levels of his medication. They found that the Dilantin level in his body was very high and that was what was causing the drowsiness. They decided to discontinue it. It had been started in May 1979, after he went into the first deep sleep, because they thought that it had been caused by an epileptic seizure. Within a few days, the drowsiness and puffiness disappeared. I was so thankful that they were able to identify the problem.

On Monday, October 6th, Marinus and Kent gave Si a beautiful blessing. I was grateful for the Priesthood that they held and honoured. I had such a feeling of love and peace come over me as Marinus was blessing Si. I felt of his spirit and the great love that he had for Si.

He blessed Si to recover from his most recent illnesses, and prayed that the doctors and nurses would be able to always determine the cause. He blessed Si with the courage to face his trials and always be an example to those around him. He told Si that his Heavenly Father loved him greatly and had a special mission for him to perform. He said that through the Priesthood's power, our Heavenly Father could heal all, if it is within his purposes to do so, but that Si must be patient and accept things in the Lord's time. He told Si that, through prayer and close communication with our Heavenly Father, he could know what our Heavenly Father's purposes were concerning him and, if he remained faithful, he would someday be with our Heavenly Father and our elder brother, Jesus Christ, again. He blessed him that he would get well and be able to do all the things that he desired to do. He also spoke of my love for Si and I could feel so strongly Marinus' love for him, too. It was a beautiful blessing and the spirit was there in rich abundance. It was a special and moving experience, and I felt privileged to be a witness to it.

On Wednesday, October 8th, they took Si completely off all medication, except for Metamucil for his bowels and an antibiotic injection twice daily for his bladder infection. As I sat by him that day, he seemed to become more uncomfortable as the day went on, and by 6:30 p.m., he was having difficulty swallowing and his body was all covered with a rash. Mrs. Dixon phoned the doctor. He came and took Si's blood gases and decided that he was having an allergic reaction to the antibiotic. He ordered it discontinued as well. Poor Si, if it wasn't one thing it was another. I was amazed at his great courage and patience through his trials. I fasted for him all the next day.

At 9:00 a.m. on Friday, October 10th, the phone rang and it was Dr. Brown calling to say that Si was having a severe seizure, and that I should come immediately. I got ready as fast as I could, all the time praying that Si would be all right. When I got there, he was just coming out of it. It started just as Jerome, the orderly, was beginning to turn him. He bit his tongue quite badly before Jerome was able to get it back into his mouth. They gave him a large dose of Dilantin and Valium through his G-tube to bring him out of it. After the seizure passed, I was amazed at how alert Si was. He could even remember what record he had on the record player. I was sure this seizure was caused because they took all of his medications away too abruptly. They should have reduced the dosages slowly.

The next day when I visited Si, I found that he was very sleepy and could barely talk to me. About 2:30 p.m. he went to sleep, and we could not wake him up. At midnight, I decided to try to wake him. I spoke to him quite loudly and shook his head gently. He opened his eyes and seemed very relaxed and calm. I think his body was just worn out from the seizure and everything else his body was going through, and just needed rest.

He was so happy when he woke up, and we had such a nice visit together while I made him comfortable for the night. They put a special nurse on to be with him all night so that I could go home to bed without worrying too much about him.

A few days later, I decided I had better cut Si's hair because it was getting very long. When I was cutting the back, I found a large scaly place that felt very soft and spongy and was oozing some matter out of it. Malcolm, the orderly, shaved around it and it turned out to be a large, open, running sore. It was very tender so Si had to lie with his head turned to the side all the time. Mrs. Dixon, Si's nurse, put a plastic bandage on it that was supposed to seal it off and make it heal more quickly. I prayed that it would heal quickly so that Si would be able to go to the opening of the Stake Center.

On Thursday, October 30th, when I was with Si, Dr. Brown came in and said that he wanted to reduce Si's volumes of air from 1100 ccs to 750 ccs. He said that they would start reducing it on Monday. I knew that it would be better for Si to breathe on lower volumes, but it was so hard to think of him having to go through the terrible suffering of shortness of breath in order to accomplish that. Si was so brave about it and assured me that he would be able to stand it. I was not sure that I would be able to, though.

We asked the people of our Ward to fast and pray for Si and their prayers were heard and answered. Si's volumes were able to be decreased to 700 ccs in one day, and he suffered no discomfort at all. Usually it would have taken about two weeks to accomplish this, and he would have suffered greatly from shortness of breath.

The sore on the back of Si's head healed very quickly, and he was actually healthier, in every way, than he had been for quite some time.

Miracles had occurred and he was able to attend the open house of our new Riverbend Stake Center.

The Open House was held from the 18th to the 24th of November 1980 and it was a great success!

The play "Within These Walls", and the variety shows that were presented, were well attended and were excellent performances. "The Si Peterson Story" was shown many times each day. From the comments received, I felt that it had touched many lives and had been the missionary tool that it was intended to be.

12
THE MIRACLE OF THE SLIDES

A remarkable experience happened with the slides for Si's story on the Tuesday after the Open House.

At the last showing of Si's story on Saturday evening, the slides in the carousel began to stick and quite a few of them had to be removed to keep it working. I decided to take it home with me and get the slides back in order and exchange some of the slides for better ones that I had at home. My sister, Eltie Helgerson, was visiting at the time and all day Monday, November 26th she helped me go through the slides and replace them in perfect order. We worked on them from 8:00 a.m. to 4:00 p.m., and as we did this, we came to really appreciate the many hours and great effort Bob Layton had put into making this slide presentation.

Bob came over in the afternoon to pick it up because he wanted to show it to some friends the next evening, but we weren't quite finished so he stayed and helped us for a while. He seemed pleased with the changes we had made. I told him that I would bring it to his home the next afternoon.

I went through the whole presentation a few more times the next day and when it was time to drop the slides off at Bob's, I felt we had an excellent presentation put together again, even better than the original, because some of the pictures of Si, before the accident, were better than the ones originally used.

This was Eltie's last day of visiting with us so she wanted to go to the mall to do some shopping. I decided to take her on the way to drop the slides off at Bob's. She helped me carry everything out to the car and, because we both had our arms full, one of us (and we still can't remember who) put the box of slides on top of the car while we got the rest of the equipment in. I remembered thinking when I saw it there, that that was a dangerous thing to do because we might forget it.

I drove Eltie to the mall and then took the Quesnel freeway to Bob's house. After unloading everything, I realized that the box with the carousel and slides was missing. I assumed we had left it in the front entry at home and told Bob I would drop it off that evening.

I left Bob's house and was just about to the Aberhart Hospital when, all of a sudden, I saw, in my mind, that yellow box on the top of the car and I realized that we had not left it in the house. When the realization of what we had done hit me, I thought I would have a nervous breakdown. I turned the car around as quickly as I could and headed for home. When I turned the corner onto our street, I could see a yellow box on the road in front of the house. My heart almost stopped beating when I realized that it was as flat as a pancake and had obviously been run over several times. I jumped out of the car and picked it up to find that it was only the top of the box. The carousel was nowhere to be found. I ran into the house and cried for Lori to come quickly and help me look for it. We left Lori's baby, Stacey, with Barbie and jumped into the car to look for the carousel and slides. We drove slowly over the same route that I had taken to drop Eltie off at the mall, and there, right in front of Avalon School, on the opposite side of the road, beside the fire hydrant, was the carousel. The slides were scattered all over the road. I stopped the car and watched in horror as two buses and a car ran over the slides right in front of us. I then parked the car across the middle of the road so that no more cars could go by, and then Lori and I got out and began to pick up the slides. I was crying so hard that I could barely see to pick them up. We got back into the car after picking up all that we could find. Seven slides were still in the carousel. The carousel was damaged from falling off the car, and we couldn't find the bottom of the box. There were ten slides missing.

As soon as we got home, I began getting the slides back in order to see which ones were missing and that was when I realized that a miracle had occurred. Although the slides had been run over several times and there were tire tracks all over the white frames of the slides, not one slide was damaged and only a few were even dirty! This truly was a miracle, and I was so very grateful to my Heavenly Father for protecting them. My heart was still heavy, however, as I found that some of the missing slides were ones of Si before his accident and thus were impossible to replace.

I phoned Bob Layton and told him what had happened and arranged to pick up the cassette player. He was very understanding and even phoned later to see how we were doing. I was so grateful for the support that Lori and all of my family were to me during this difficult time.

Lori fixed supper, Marinus picked Eltie up at the mall, and then Eltie helped me sort through the slides and get them into a new carousel in the right sequence. We worked on it until 9:30 p.m. and then I went up to be with Si. I stayed with him until midnight. On the way home I decided to stop by Avalon school to see if I could find any more of the slides. The streetlights were really bright in front of the school so I could see clearly. I carefully combed the whole area in front of the school, and on the lawn right next to the school, I found seven more slides, including all but one of the slides of Si before his accident. The other two that were still missing were ones that we had duplicates of.

My heart was so full of gratitude to my Heavenly Father for hearing and answering my prayers. This was a testimony to me that this presentation was important and that "The Si Peterson Story" was, and would continue to be, an influence for good in the lives of many people, and was preserved for this very special purpose.

I am grateful for this incident in my life and that I was able to witness another modern-day miracle.

The Si Peterson Story

They can because they think they can

"The Si Peterson Story" was shown many times in the Catholic High School where Bob Layton's daughter was a student. Bob showed it during a religion class that was held in the gym. The first time Bob went there to show it, there were several of the male students sitting at the very back of the gym. The teacher told Bob that they would probably sneak out before he was finished, but not to worry, because that is what they always did whenever they had a guest come to their class.

Bob showed the slide show and when it was over, those boys were not only still there but they were obviously very moved by Si's story.

The class was 45 minutes long and Si's story only took 30 minutes so Bob asked the teacher (a Catholic Nun) what he should do for the remainder of the time. She told him to answer any questions that the students might have. They asked many questions about Si's faith, and Bob was able to teach them about their Heavenly Father and the Plan of Salvation. The blessing that Si had received from Brother Patterson, shortly after his accident happened, that told Si that through him many people who didn't know Heavenly Father, would come to know Him, was certainly fulfilled in the lives of these young people. Many of the students wrote letters to Si, thanking him for his faith and for his great example.

In December 1980, Si got severe pneumonia. It just didn't seem to get any better so the doctors decided to do a bronchoscopy on him. The doctors felt it was necessary to go down into his lungs and clean them out. It was quite a long procedure, and I'm sure it was a very uncomfortable one for Si. I was glad that his friend, Darlene, a nurse from ICU days, was the one who did it for him. She was a special person who really cared for Si. She was able to clean his lungs out very thoroughly, and he felt much better.

Because Si was a little better, I decided to go to Victoria with my husband to attend the wedding of Marinus' niece and the 25th wedding anniversary of Marinus' sister and her husband.

I phoned Si each night while I was away, and one night as I talked with him, I felt that all was not well and I knew that he wished that I was home with him. He was suffering long bouts of shortness of breath, and this is a terrible thing to bear alone. One night about midnight, Leigh Ann phoned with the message that Si was not well and that I should come home as soon as possible. I wasn't sure if I could get a flight out because we were not planning on coming home for a few more days. I told Leigh Ann that I would try to get a flight the next morning. I was not able to get a flight until 3:00 p.m. arriving in Edmonton at 9:00 p.m. I was disappointed that I would be getting into Edmonton so late but was thankful that I was able to go. Leigh Ann and Benjie picked me up at the airport and I went directly to the hospital. Si was so very pleased and relieved to see me. After I bagged him for a little while, his breathing became much easier.

Christmas was wonderful that year, as usual, but especially wonderful because Si's health had finally improved enough that he was able to be home with us for the entire Christmas holiday. Si recorded the following about it in his journal.

I came home for the holidays on Christmas Eve. We had our Christmas dinner that night as usual, and Mom invited many people to share it with us. After dinner we had our Family Home Evening. Mom read the story of Jesus' birth from the Bible and the kids took their different parts, but they didn't dress up this year. The members of the family told incidents from Jesus' life that had influenced their lives. We sang a few Christmas carols too. After Family Home Evening, we watched 'Mr. Krueger's Christmas' on TV.

13
MORE TRIALS

We took Si to the New Year's Eve dance at the Riverbend Stake Center. He was able to stay until almost the end of the dance. During the evening, Leslie (Si's step sister) sang with the band and dedicated the Beetles' song "Hey Jude" to Si. He was very pleased that she acknowledged him.

We had recently had a new reconditioned motor put in our van. On our way to the dance, smoke was pouring out of the back of the van and, just as we got there, it began to overheat. Another problem with "our lemon"! We were all wondering how we were going to get back home, but with Dad B's help, the lemon made it home. I sure was glad to get home because I wasn't feeling very well. I was just getting over a case of pneumonia.

Si stayed at home with us for the whole week after Christmas. He was still not in very good health and kept experiencing severe shortness of breath. I don't know why his life always had to be so hard, but he certainly was an example in the way that he so patiently bore his trials and discomforts. I sat by him for many hours and stroked his hair. It seemed to make him feel better.

My Home Teachers came today. They are David Kuzminski and Rick Nielson. They read a bulletin from the Bishopric to me. It told all about the things that happened in our Stake last year. The bulletin reminded us of important things that need to be completed this year, such as our Four Generation Geneology sheets and our personal histories. The bulletin ended with a quote from the 1939 Christmas message from King George VI, "I said to the man who stood at the gate of the year, 'Give me a light that I may tread safely into the unknown'. And he replied, 'Go out into the darkness and put your hand into the hand of God. That is better than a light and safer than a known way'."

Si continued to have a bad infection in his lungs as the days went by and required a great deal of suctioning. He was not feeling at all well. The mucus in his lungs was very thick and had a very strong odour. I spoke with Dr. Brown, and he decided to do some more tests on Si to try to determine what kind of bug was growing in his lungs. He said that it could just be pseudomonas bacteria, and if it was, Si would just have to live with it.

I have been very sick with pneumonia since just after the New Year. What happened was, a germ called pseudomonas began growing in my lungs. It has a very foul odor. The doctor tried to treat it with penicillin, but it just kept getting worse. It got so bad that I could hardly breathe. Finally, they found out what was causing me to be so sick. It was an anaerobic germ that is really hard to culture. They began giving me massive doses of penicillin (2 to 3 million units per day). It helped to some degree. The odour decreased greatly, but I still wasn't able to breathe very well. My lungs bled quite badly on two occasions, which caused Dr. Brown to call in specialists from the Infectious Diseases Department of the University Hospital. After taking more tests, they decided to stop the penicillin and gave me two different antibiotics by injection. These injections were very effective and I seemed to get much better right away. My breathing became easier, my secretions cleared up, and the odour disappeared. I still felt very tired and weak though, because my blood count was quite low from the infection.

One night about midnight, as I was getting ready to go home from Si, he needed suctioning. The nurse came in to suction him and as she did this, his lungs began to bleed quite badly. They called the doctor, and a new resident came. He took blood gases and checked Si over. The bleeding subsided so they decided not to take him to the ICU. He became very short of breath so I stayed with him until 1:30 a.m. He was calm and feeling a little better when I left.

The next day he was still feeling quite ill and was constantly short of breath. His neck was hurting quite badly, and his whole body seemed to be very stiff and spastic. His temperature was up, and the nurses were putting cold, wet towels on him to bring it down. I stayed with Si all day and did my best to help him be comfortable. It was so hard to see him suffer so badly and not be able to do very much for him. He was always so brave through it all and rarely complained. I don't know how he stood the shortness of breath. I am sure that if I was him,

I would have lost my mind long ago. I know he was blessed by our Heavenly Father, or I am sure he couldn't have stood it either.

Marinus was in Ottawa on business so Bishop Hudson and Brother Takahashi came and gave Si a beautiful blessing. They rebuked the disease and told Si that his life would be spared so that he could fulfill his mission here upon the earth. They blessed him with strength to overcome his illness and to be strong through the trials he had to face. I know the blessing brought comfort to Si. His smile of gratitude really touched my heart. How grateful I was for this fine, brave son. I sat by Si the rest of the day, stroking his hair and trying to bring him comfort through his long periods of shortness of breath. He was able to go to sleep about midnight so I went home.

The next day, Mrs. Zorsus, a nurse at the hospital, called telling me that Si's lung was bleeding again and he was very upset and for me to come quickly. When I got there, the nurses were sponging him with cold towels, because his fever had spiked. He was very short of breath because his heart was racing at about 140 beats a minute. I sat by him and stroked his hair and bagged him quite often and soon his heart rate became slower and he calmed down. It was so hard to see him suffer so much and not be able to do much for him. I was just very grateful that he felt secure with me and was able to become calmer when I was with him.

Si was not able to go to his meetings on Sunday, but he thought he would be all right until I could come back to him after Church.

During our meetings, a nurse from the hospital phoned our home and Benjie, who was home sick with a sore throat, phoned the church to give me the message. Si was really ill again, and I was needed at the hospital. When I got there, I found that he was having a really hard time getting enough air. His volumes and pressure were quite high, but his lungs were so congested that they hardly moved at all. I bagged him quite hard for a long time, but this just didn't seem to help at all. His lips and his fingernails were quite blue. The doctor came in and looked at him and ordered an x-ray. An x-ray was taken to see if his lung had perforated. It had not, but his lungs were full of pneumonia. I did Si's installation and I cannot believe the gross matter that came out of his lungs. I suggested to the nurse that perhaps he needed some extra oxygen added into his line. They tried to do it with compressed air and the sudden increase in volume almost blew his lungs out. I didn't see why they couldn't just put it directly into his line like they did in the ICU. I decided to talk to the respiratory technician about it the next day.

They did extensive blood work on Si, and then gave him massive doses of penicillin – 2 to 3 million units per day — which seemed to help a little. The smell disappeared from Si's secretions, but they were still very thick and yellow. They gave Si a little extra oxygen straight into his tubing. They also gave him a treatment with a side stream of medication every 4 to 6 hours. Si's lips got quite blue whenever he felt shortness of breath, and his fingernails were also becoming quite clubbed, which was also an indication that he was not getting enough oxygen.

The extensive blood work that was done on Si showed that, besides pseudomonas, he was also growing an anaerobic germ. They were able to culture it and continued treating it with large doses of penicillin. Si continued to be very sick. His heart kept racing for no apparent reason, causing him to become extremely short of breath. This frightened him, which caused his heart to beat even faster. It was a vicious cycle. It got so bad one night that they did an ECG on him. However, it didn't show anything abnormal. The infectious disease specialist from the U of A Hospital came and did some tests on Si, and asked a lot of questions about him. They decided to change his medications and began giving him 2 strong antibiotics by injection, 2 in his hip and 1 in his arm, every 6 hours. One of the antibiotics was a new drug that was clearing up lung infections in cystic fibrosis patients.

One night when I went to leave Si at about 11:00 p.m., he seemed very apprehensive. He wouldn't tell me exactly what was bothering him, but I felt he was afraid of being alone at night with his shortness of breath, so I asked him if he would like me to stay all night with him. He seemed so happy and relieved when I suggested that, so I was thankful that I was able to stay. The orderly brought me a chair from the lounge so I would be more comfortable.

Si was quite short of breath, so I sat by him and stroked his hair until he finally fell asleep around midnight. I settled down in the chair and was just beginning to doze off when the orderly and two nurses came in to turn Si. They were really noisy when they came in. The orderly shone his flashlight in Si's face and then turned on the overhead light. Their noise and the lights being turned on so abruptly startled me and really upset Si. He started having bad spasms and his stomach muscles were really jerking. Si was lying on his side, facing the door, and wanted to be turned on to his back instead of right over onto his right side because he had difficulty breathing while lying on that side. He clicked to tell the orderly what to do and the orderly ignored him and proceeded to turn him right over. Si clicked again — still no acknowledgment. Finally, I told the orderly what Si wanted and he didn't seem too happy about complying with Si's wishes. After they turned him, the orderly decided that Si needed to be suctioned. He put sterile gloves on both hands and then proceeded to fill the suction basin and change the suction bottle and get a catheter ready. He then, with those contaminated gloves, began to suction Si. He kept the suction hose in Si's lung so long, Si began to be in some distress. He finally put Si's trach back on, and then, without even letting him have a breath, he began suctioning again. This time, Si was really having trouble and was fighting for air. When the orderly was going to repeat this the third time, I told him that Si had had enough suctioning. He didn't agree with me and didn't like my interference, but at least he stopped. By the time they all had left the room, Si was so upset that his heart was beating 150 beats per minute, and he was extremely short of breath. It took over an hour of sitting by him, stroking his hair and occasionally bagging him, to finally get him calm enough so he could sleep again.

I could not believe what had just gone on and was truly amazed that Si had been able to put up with this for so long without complaining. I sat back down in my chair and was just getting comfortable when I realized that, in less than an hour, they would be back in to repeat this whole procedure again. I just couldn't let this happen so I went out to the nurse and told her that I would turn Si and suction him when he needed it, for the rest of the night. She offered to help me turn Si but I told her I could manage just fine because I did it all the time when Si was at home. Si had a good sleep the rest of the night. I turned him at 3:00 a.m., 5:00 a.m. and 7:00 a.m. without waking him. When the day staff came in at 8:00 a.m. to do his installation, they couldn't believe how well he looked and how happy and cheerful he was. I waited to go home until I had the opportunity to talk with the charge nurse about the events of the night. She was really appalled and said that she would talk to the staff about it. When I left for home about 10:00 a.m., Si was feeling better and resting comfortably.

The new drugs that they gave Si were truly miracle drugs because the infection in his lungs cleared up, and his breathing became much easier. He felt so much better and was eager to start doing things again. It was wonderful to see him well and able to enjoy life.

14
KNIT ONE AND PEARL TWO

One morning when I went up to Si, the nurse met me in the hall and asked me if I could put Si's G-tube (the gastrointestinal tube in his stomach that he was fed through) back in. Apparently, it got pulled out during his bath and no one could get a new one back in. The doctor was not able to come right then, and the charge nurse tried to do it, but couldn't. There seemed to be some resistance when she tried to push it in and she was afraid to push very hard. Everything was set up and ready so I put it in. It is really a very simple procedure, but very scary if you haven't done it before. Fortunately I'd had some previous experience installing stomach tubes.

About a year after Si's accident happened, he was home and, as I was undressing him, I pulled out his stomach tube. I phoned the hospital to see if they would send someone to our home to put it back in. They said that they couldn't do that and that I should bring Si back to the hospital to have it reinserted. Food was pouring out of Si's stomach so I didn't know how I was ever going to get him dressed again and taken back to the Aberhart. I had never changed his g-tube before, but I had seen it done many times. I was a little hesitant about doing it, but Si assured me that I would be able to do it just fine.

I put the tube in some boiling water to sterilize it, and then I wondered what I could use to insert it with. In the hospital they used a long thing called a stylus, but I didn't have one of those at home. I thought about it for a minute and then I decided that a knitting needle would work just as well, so I found one and sterilized it, too.

I felt a little squeamish when I had to put the tube into the hole in his stomach, but I swallowed hard and did it.

I phoned the hospital to tell them that I had put it in and everything was fine.

The next day when I went up to the hospital the nurses said to me, "We understand that you 'knit one and pearled two' and put Si back together again!"

Sunday, March 15, 1981 – Mom woke me at 7:45 a.m. to do my installation and get me ready for church. Benjie and Leigh Ann helped Mom lift me into my chair. As Mom was taking me backwards down the ramp in the front entry, Benjie pulled on the foot-rests so the chair wouldn't go too fast and run over Mom. One of the foot-rests came off and Benjie lost his hold. The chair and I were a little too heavy for Mom to hold, so it went down really fast and nearly ran over Mom. She got quite a bump. We couldn't help but laugh, but I'm not sure if Mom thought it was so funny.

April 12, 1981 - Today is my 23rd birthday. The staff all came in and sang 'Happy Birthday' to me, and brought me a birthday cake. (Today is the day they launched the space shuttle from Cape Canaveral. They tried to do it yesterday but it failed.)

I spent the day at home and for supper we had all my favourite foods — ham, baked potatoes, sour cream, hot bean salad, corn, and pineapple glump. For dessert we had cherry cake with almond icing. That evening, after Family Home Evening, we opened my gifts and cards, and had cake and ice cream.

15
EDUCATION WEEK

For the closing of Education Week, that was held in May of 1981, they showed "The Si Peterson Story". After showing it, Bob Layton called all the lecturers up and presented them with a small remembrance of Edmonton. He then asked Si if he would bear his testimony before offering the closing prayer. Si bore a beautiful testimony and then offered a simple and beautiful prayer. Everyone was really moved by the spirit that was there. Many of those that had spoken at Education Week came up to Si and expressed their love for him and said that they had gained much from his example of courage and faith. Sister Ardeth Kapp and Sister Lucille Johnson — two of the presenters — both shed tears and kissed him and told him how much they loved and admired him. It was a beautiful end to a beautiful week.

The first time Sister Kapp met Si was when she had come to Edmonton to be the guest speaker at our Stake Youth Conference. She was in the General Young Women's Presidency at the time. I was taking Si to the conference and as we were going into the Bonnie Doon Stake Center, Sister Kapp held the door open for me as I pushed Si's chair through. When we got into the foyer, she came over to Si and said, "Young man I don't know who you are, but I want you to know that your spirit is glowing outside of your body." This was an amazing and wonderful experience for Si and it helped us to realize that, although Si's body was completely handicapped, his spirit was not. It was free to grow and increase as he strived to keep the commandments and do all that his Heavenly Father expected of him.

A few weeks later, Si received a letter and a package from Sister Kapp. The package contained a compilation of articles on the philosophy of trials. I read these articles to him many times over the years, and he received great strength from them. She later became the Matron of the Cardston, Alberta Temple, when her husband was called as the Temple President. Whenever I would see her there she would talk to me about Si and wonder if he would be allowed to be in the Temple with us that day.

THE CHURCH OF JESUS CHRIST OF LATTER-DAY SAINTS
OFFICE OF THE PRESIDING BISHOPRIC
THE YOUNG WOMEN
50 EAST NORTH TEMPLE STREET
SALT LAKE CITY, UTAH 84150

February 17, 1976

Mr. Si Peterson
5819 - 114 "A" Street
Edmonton, Alberta
Canada

Dear Si:

   Among the many wonderful opportunities I had while visiting
Edmonton I am grateful for the privilege I had of meeting you and
your Mom and your friend Cam.

   Upon my return I spoke to Bishop Featherstone about you and
he remembered about trying to arrange his schedule while he was in
Edmonton so he might meet you personally. He told me that upon his
return he had put your name on the prayer roll in the Salt Lake Temple.
He rejoiced in getting the report of the wonderful spirit which you
and your mother radiate to all those who have the privilege of coming
within your influence. Although you seemed to radiate an attitude of
calm, quiet assurance and abiding testimony, still I am sure there are
days that the burden becomes heavy and an easing of that burden would
be most welcome. I have in my file a document compiled by a young man
who underwent extreme adversity in his young life through severe burns.
This compilation is his work, and I have found it to be a marvelous
assortment of "references and scriptural truths" which put the purpose
and meaning of life in its true perspective. I am enclosing a copy of
this document in hopes you might also find it conforting and uplifting.

   May the Lord continue to bless you and your Mom as you, by your
example, are such a powerful example and influence for good to many of
us including your friend Cam. Extend my best wishes to him also. Among
all of the youth I was privileged to meet while in Edmonton, you stand
out as the ones that enriched and strengthened my life.

   May you be blessed as you meet the challenges of each day during this
brief mortal period as we think of it in reference to the eternal nature
of we who are our Father's sons and daughters.

Most sincerely,

Ardeth G. Kapp
The Young Women General Presidency

AGK/gm
Encls.

He also received the following beautiful letter from Sister Ruth H.
Funk, the General President of Young Women

THE CHURCH OF JESUS CHRIST OF LATTER-DAY SAINTS
OFFICE OF THE PRESIDING BISHOPRIC
THE YOUNG WOMEN
50 EAST NORTH TEMPLE STREET
SALT LAKE CITY, UTAH 84150

November 30, 1976

Brother Si Peterson
5819 - 114 "A" Street
Edmonton, Alberta, Canada

Dear Si:

It is difficult for me to erase from my mind the beautiful image
of love and patience portrayed by you and your sweet mother as I
visited with you while in Edmonton last weekend. I had heard so much
about you from Sister Kapp and President Tanner, and yet seeing you
and meeting you in person gave a new dimension to my understanding.
I knew that you would reflect courage, but I don't believe that I have
ever witnessed or felt such a strong emotion of love as I felt in your
presence.

My visit to Edmonton and the opportunity of participating in the
outstanding Mothers and Daughters Conference will always be remembered
as a highlight in my life. Then my visit to you, climaxed it all.

Normally the Christmas season would present a very dismal pros-
pect to someone who has the problems you have, but having met you
I have visions that you will make Christmas a memorable occasion for
everyone you know--just by your spirit and great love.

May the Lord continue to bless you as you touch the lives of your
friends and associates in a very special way. You may be assured that
any subsequent visit to Edmonton will be incomplete without dropping
into your room to be refreshed and rejuvenated.

Gratefully,

Ruth H. Funk
General President of Young Women

RHF:MB

P. S. Sister Kapp sends her regards. I will remember you to President
Tanner when I meet him next time.

How grateful I was for people like Sister Kapp and Sister Funk whose love and concern for Si lifted him to greater heights.

16

THE IKEA ADVENTURE and
THE NEWSPAPER ARTICLE

On Monday, June 1 1981, Leigh Ann and Eric (Leigh Ann's boy-friend) and I took Si to Ikea to look at wall units for his room. We found one Si liked and loaded it into the van, but when Eric tried to start the van it wouldn't go. The steering had been very loose on the van for some time, and I felt that it just wasn't safe to drive. I believe Heavenly Father caused the starter to break so we couldn't drive it. This did present a problem for us though, because I had no way to get Si back to the hospital. I phoned DATS but they would not come unless we were a member. They did give me the number of a ParaVan, however. I phoned them and they were running about an hour behind schedule with their last pickup around 2:30 p.m. I gave them our information and asked them to pick us up, but that I would phone them back if I found someone that could pick us up sooner. I then phoned the hospital, but both vans were in use. I phoned Marinus' office to ask him what I should do about the van, but he wasn't there. While we were waiting, I pushed Si down to a Kelly's music store to look at records. We bought two. When we got back to IKEA, the girl told us that Marinus had called. I called him back and Marinus arranged for the AMA to tow the van to a garage to be repaired. Leigh Ann and Eric began walking down the freeway to catch a bus home. Si and I began our waiting game.

I plugged Si's respirator in at the IKEA store so his battery wouldn't go dead. We waited and waited. At 4:45 p.m., I decided I had better call and see why they hadn't come yet. The fellow that answered the phone had no record of my call, but said he would come as soon as possible. He finally did arrive, and we got back to the hospital at 5:30 p.m.

I could not believe how well Si was through all of this. He hadn't needed to be tipped back or suctioned once the whole time, and he wasn't even tired. I am grateful to my Heavenly Father for His protection over us, and for blessing Si with such good health again.

Wednesday, December 16, 1981 - *Today a reporter for the Edmonton Journal, Agnes Butner, came to interview me and my Mom for an article they want to do about me and my family for the paper. She talked with us for over 2 hours, and my Mom was able to tell her all about our beliefs and faith. We don't know how much she will put in her article, but she wanted to know everything. A photographer also came with her and took a few pictures.*

Tuesday, December 22, 1981 - *The article about me and Mom was in the Journal today. Our picture and the article were on the front page! I thought it would probably be put on the last page. When my Mom was grocery shopping today she was walking by a newspaper stand and saw the paper. She was really surprised and quite startled to see our picture on the very front page!*

Wednesday, December 23, 1981 - *The missionaries who serve in our Ward came up to visit me today. They told me that while they were tracting yesterday they were invited into the home of an elderly man who couldn't read, and they had the opportunity to read the article that was in the Journal, to him. He was really interested in it when they told him that they belonged to the same church as I did.*

Also today, an elderly man, who saw my picture in the paper, came to see me. He phoned my mom and asked if he could visit and play his fiddle for me. He is a very interesting man! He told us how he taught himself to play the violin even though he cannot read music. He is still playing on the same old violin that he got when he was 11 years old. He is now almost 70. He played and sang a cute little song for me entitled "Don't You Worry". He gave me a copy of the words and Mom wrote them in my journal for me. The author of it is unknown.

"There's a town called Don't-You-Worry on the banks of the river Smile,
Where the Cheer-up and Be-Happy blossom all the while.
Where the Never-Grumble flowers bloom beside the Fragrant -Try,
And the Don't-Give-up and Patience point their faces to the sky.
In the Valley of Contentment, in the Province of I-Will,

You will find this lovely city at the foot of No-Fret hill.
There are thoroughfares delightful in this truly charming town,
And on every hand are shade trees, named Very-Seldom-Frown.
Rustic benches, quite enticing, you'll find scattered here and there,
And to each a vine is clinging, called the Frequent-Earnest-Prayer.
Everybody here is happy, and is singing all the while,
In the town of Don't You Worry, on the banks of the river Smile."

I enjoyed his visit and appreciated the time he spent with me. It really made my day!

Bob Layton and his family came up tonight and brought me the plate that the front page of the Journal was printed from. Bob said he had to search through a lot of old plates to find this one. I appreciated his thoughtfulness in doing this for me. He is such a good friend.

17

A NEW VAN

The month of March 1982 was quite a difficult month for us. Si's lift broke on his van so we had to use the ramps again, and this was very difficult because of the ice and snow. Then the transmission went on the van, so for a few weeks we had to rent a van to take Si out.

When we went over our money, it seemed utterly impossible for us to pay for a new van, but Marinus spent many, many hours going over all the pros and cons of the situation, and he was finally able to come up with a solution. I really felt that he was inspired, that our prayers were heard and answered, as he was able to work things out in a wise and efficient way.

We decided to borrow some money from the bank, using our home as collateral. With the money we were able to purchase a van, a new lift and seat belts to hold Si's chair in place. We sold our old van for $1,750 dollars. Frank agreed to pay for Si's lift and we really appreciated that.

Marinus spent many hours looking for a new van. I am sure he visited every van dealership in Edmonton, but he wanted to make sure he made the best deal. I went with him quite often, and I was really amazed at his ability to wheel and deal. We finally found a black, 1981 Dodge Van at Crosstown Motors. Because it was last year's stock, they were selling it at the cost price of $9,400. I couldn't believe my ears when Marinus very calmly said to the salesman, "I will give you $9,200 for it if you put in a cruise control." The salesman looked like he didn't believe what he had heard either and said his superiors would never go for that. The salesman presented Marinus' offer to his boss and, believe it or not, he accepted it! I was so amazed at Marinus' audacity and his brilliant performance that I could hardly contain myself.

We got ourselves a brand new beautiful van with a cruise control for $9,200 Unbelievable! (Remember, this is 1982!)

We were then faced with the problem of getting the van upholstered, insulated, and carpeted. We finally decided to see what Apex Auto Upholstery had to offer. Apex was owned by Edmonton's mayor, Cecil Purves, who was a member of our church and a really good friend. The business was run by Bob Gilson and Cecil's son-in-law, Randy Lybbert, who were also members of the church. When Marinus talked to Bob Gilson, he said that, because the van was for Si, Apex would do the entire interior for us at cost. Another miracle! They put in four windows and completely insulated and upholstered it for us. They even put in a beautiful captain's chair for me to sit in beside Si. We bought some carpet and they installed it for us, too. The van was really beautiful and had everything in it for Si's comfort and safety.

How blessed we were, and how very grateful I was for my wonderful husband, who continually showed his great love for Si in so many ways. We knew that as long as we paid an honest tithing, our Heavenly Father would continue to pour out His blessings upon us and we would always be able to meet our obligations and provide adequately for ourselves and others.

On May 15, 1982, Marinus, Si and I went to the Bonnie Doon Stake Centre to show Si's Story to the youth of that Stake in the closing exercises of their Youth Conference. Sandy Burnham was in charge and she introduced Si to all the young people there. I explained a little bit about Si's story and then it was shown. After showing it, Si bore his testimony and then all these young people stood and unaccompanied, sang "I Am a Child of God". It was so beautiful and there was such a sweet spirit there that I just stood and cried. After they finished singing, President Blair Bennett, of their Stake Presidency, presented Si with a beautiful parchment scroll on which was written, "A Tribute to Si Peterson". Over 200 young people had signed it. What a thoughtful and touching gift!

Experiences like this were so precious and important in Si's life. How grateful I was for wonderful people who constantly built him up and helped him feel of worth. Things like this made me realize, more than ever, the very special mission Si had been called to fulfill. He was touching many lives and influencing them for good.

18
THE TEMPLE

Tuesday, June 8, 1982 – Mom and Dad B took me for my temple interview with President Salmon this evening. After my interview, Mom came in and Pres. Salmon talked to us about the temple ceremony and gave me a little booklet about the temple that he asked me to read before I went to the temple on the 22nd of June. He counselled me to always try to fill my mind with uplifting thoughts, especially during those times when I was alone with only my thoughts.

President Salmon also told us that there was about 900 dollars left over from the money the primary children saved for my lift and he wanted to know if we could use it. This was an answer to prayer because we really needed some money as we had just purchased a new van.

Shortly after my accident happened, the Primary children of our stake decided to save their pennies and instead of sending them to the primary children's hospital in Salt Lake, they decided to use it to buy a lift for me for our van. They collected over $2,400 in about 8 months and completely paid for my lift besides having, as we learned today, a surplus of $900. I am very grateful for their thoughtfulness in doing this for me. Before we got the lift, we had to use ramps to get me into the van and this was quite difficult.

On Friday, June 18th, 1982, we traveled to Southern Alberta for Si's holiday. David and Benjie traveled with us. We arrived at Eltie's quite late but she had everything ready for us so it didn't take us long to get settled in. Our new van ran so beautifully. How grateful we were to have such safe transportation for Si, at last. He had an excellent trip and didn't even seem tired when we arrived.

We had a long busy day the next day attending my niece's wedding and when we got Si back to Eltie's late that night, he went into a deep sleep again, and we couldn't wake him. We didn't panic this time. We were sure that it was happening because he was so tired from traveling and being out all day. When I turned him the second time in the night, he finally responded. It was a remarkable thing the way his body took care of itself and knew what to do to be revitalized.

On Monday, June 21st, we had Family Home Evening in Lethbridge at the home of my cousin Dennis Bullock and his wife Carol. We showed the Si Peterson Story and I told a few faith-promoting stories surrounding Si's accident. It was a wonderful evening. There was a sweet spirit there.

Monday, June 21st — This morning, Dad B gave me a priesthood blessing in preparation for going to the temple tomorrow. It was a very special blessing and we recorded it on a little tape recorder and Mom transcribed it into my journal...

"Frank Siedel Peterson, by the power of the holy Melchizedek Priesthood, which I hold, and in the name of Jesus Christ, I pronounce upon you a priesthood blessing. As one of those that are close to you in your life, it is a privilege for me to function as your father. You now have two fathers in your life in your earthly existence. I counsel you to always give honour to your Dad Peterson.

You are a special young man who has shown great patience and understanding of the purpose of our existence here and you will continue to be a great inspiration to many. I say unto you that your mind will be calm as you will be entering that very sacred building tomorrow morning. I bless you that your body functions will perform as they should and that you will be well as you enter the temple. I bless you with the ability to understand and to receive joy in taking out your personal endowment tomorrow morning. You will be blessed with great understanding of the purposes of the Kingdom as they will be unfolding as the sacred dialogue will commence in the endowment session. I bless you that you will be able to speak clearly so that those that will be assisting you, as you go through the temple, will be able to read your lips. There will not be any discomfort to any that will be participating. I bless you, Si, with the ability to go forth and to continue to serve your Father in Heaven, as you have been doing for quite a number of years, in such an exemplary way. You are a choice spirit and have been chosen from the beginning of time to come forth at this time to serve your Father in Heaven and to stand as the valiant ones in the last days. The day will come that you will see your Saviour yet in this life and you will be there to provide comfort and strength to the brothers and sisters that will be on the earth at that time. I bless you with health and strength and energy. Your life will be preserved and you will be protected as you continue to serve your Father in Heaven on this earth. Take the time, Si, to listen to your mother before you go into the temple and she will explain to you the things you need to know. The priesthood is all-powerful and will in due time make you whole again. You do not need to be reminded that you will be able to walk and talk like us when the time comes that you will pass on into the next life. Your great faith and under-standing of these things that are true will be a constant reminder to those that come in contact with you, that there is a spirit as well as a physical body that all of us have been given, and special understanding will come to those that are not members of the church. When they come into your presence, they will feel that.

You are so special to us, Si. You are such a great example. Be faithful and let the spirit that is within you always penetrate any negative things that may come to your mind like they do to all of us. Strive to do what is right. You are very many hours each day alone and therefore have the special opportunity to commune with the spirit. This will prepare you for a special mission that I do not have the authority to give you details on at this time. But I want to tell you that a special mission is in store for you. Great will be your blessings as you share this fine spirit with others in this life and especially in the life to come. We are so very close to the veil as we commune with our Heavenly Father in times like these and you are so privileged to be so close to the veil many times, which is incomprehensible to us but which you will have a great understanding of. As you enter the holy temple, the physical representation of that veil will be shown to you. I seal these blessings upon your head and I do it humbly as one that has come close to you, as one that has been privileged to be part of your life, in the name of Jesus Christ, our Saviour, our elder brother, Amen."

Tuesday, June 22nd — We got up this morning at 4:30 a.m. to get ready to go to the temple. Mom washed my hair outside by the house in about 2 minutes flat as we were on our way to the van. We picked up David and Lori and Brian at Lori's house at 6:00 a.m. We had family prayer before we left. David had recently returned from his mission to Finland and Dad B. asked him to offer the prayer for us. He gave a beautiful prayer. We arrived in Cardston and Kenden Eakett, Brian's brother, was there at the temple to help lift me up the front stairs of the temple. He didn't attend the session with us because he had to work, but I am grateful to him for coming down to help lift me.

On the way to the temple, Mom told me a little bit about what would happen in the temple today.

Dad B showed me around the reception area. There was a really beautiful display of the last supper by Michelangelo on a table. Each character had a lot of expression on its face.

Dad B, Brian and David took me through the initiatory ceremony. I was grateful that Brian could be there to help me too. It went really smoothly. Afterward, President Wood, the President of the Temple, spoke to me briefly and explained what would be happening. He used to be our Stake Patriarch and gave me my patriarchal blessing. Pres. Wood took me all through the endowment session and did all the things for me that I could not do myself. Dad B, David, President Wood and another temple worker lifted me from level to level. I think it was really great of President Wood to do this for me because he had recently gone through a serious kidney operation. Dad B said he insisted on lifting me. The whole session went very smoothly even though there were a lot of people there. I was really pleased that my relatives, Uncle Alvin, Uncle Ray and Aunt Julia, Uncle Ernie and Aunt Millie, Uncle George and Aunt Mary, Aunt Eltie and Brother and Sister Eakett could be there with me too.

I felt a bit confused about some of the things that went on but, in the Celestial room, President Wood answered my questions for me.

I feel really thankful to my Dad B for having the faith that I would be able to go through the temple and for all he did to help make this possible.

After the session, we took some pictures in front of the temple and then we went downtown to an ice cream shop and got 2 ice cream cones each!

What a gloriously, joyful experience it was to be in the Temple with my husband and three of our children. My heart overflowed with gratitude and great joy that my Si was able to experience receiving his own endowment and could be there in that beautiful place with us. This was a fulfillment of a righteous desire — one that would not have been possible if I had not married Marinus.

Pres. Wood allowed us to stay in the Celestial room for quite some time and then we all went down to show Si the sealing room where Marinus and I were married and sealed.

19

THE STROKE

Friday, December 3, 1982 – *This morning Mom came to visit me before she was going to leave to go to the temple. My eyes were hurting and I wasn't feeling very well but I told her to go and I would be all right. Mom left and about a half hour later Mrs. von Busse, my physiotherapist, phoned my mom and asked her to come up to the hospital. I was so glad that she phoned and caught my mom before she left because during that time my eyes had gone completely blind. My blood pressure kept going very, very high for some reason and had caused me to have a stroke. My mom and dad B came up immediately and stayed with me.*

Kelly, the respiratory nurse's little girl, came in to see me. She didn't know I couldn't see her so she did some of her ballet dance for me. She is such a cute little girl and she comes in to see me whenever her mom brings her to the hospital. I wish I could have seen her little dance.

The ophthalmologist came in the afternoon and did some tests on my eyes. They could find nothing physically wrong with them except that I couldn't see. They were puzzled about it all. Dad P came at 9:30 p.m. so mom and dad B left to get something to eat. While they were gone, I suddenly became confused and could not speak clearly or express myself coherently. Dad P phoned mom and they came back up immediately. I don't remember much of the rest of that day or night.

Saturday, December 4, 1982 – Mom stayed with me all last night until noon today and Dad P left about 3:00 a.m. At 7:00 this morning Dad B came up to give me a blessing. It was a beautiful blessing in which, through the priesthood which he holds, he blessed me to be healed. He said that I would be healed completely through the power of the priesthood and not by anything the doctors would find or do. Dad P came up at noon and mom went home to get some sleep. While she was gone, my eyesight began to return and by 4:00 p.m., I could see quite well again. I still had a hard time thinking of words I wanted to say and being able to express them. My face was quite paralyzed on the right side and I had a hard time forming the words so that people could read my lips. Mom stayed with me until quite late and then they had a nurse come down from one of the other floors to work on our floor so that one of the nurses could be with me in the night.

The doctors have decided that I had a stroke caused from a clot that got away at my break site but my mom and Della, the charge nurse, are sure it was caused by the high blood pressure I had as a result of my bowel being impacted, causing my body to go through a lot of stress. They are going to do some tests tomorrow so the doctors can determine the cause. I am very thankful that my eyesight has been restored and I know I will recover completely because of the blessing I received.

My mom bore her testimony in church today and told every one of my miraculous healing and my eyesight being restored.

Thursday, December 9, 1982 – *I went to the University Hospital today for a cat scan of my head. They found that I had had quite a lot of haemorrhaging at the base of my brain and it had caused the stroke.*

Friday, December 10, 1982 – *I went to the University Hospital again today for an angiogram. Mom went with me and bagged me while they were doing it. They found that all my arteries and veins are clear. I was relieved to hear this because it meant that my stroke was not caused from a blood clot.*

(Excerpts from Si's journals and from my journals)

December 10, 1982 - This evening, Mom and Dad B picked me up for the ward Christmas party. The Kohlruss family that we are friend-shipping came to it too. My Mom and I were in charge of the background music for the banquet. We taped a lot of nice Christmas music and they played it while we were eating. I am very grateful for the power of the priesthood that healed me so that I was able to see again and was able to go to the party.

Kent came up to read to me earlier today. While he was here, one of the housekeeping staff, Betty Melvin, came into my room. I have been trying to ask her if she would like to take the discussions but she cannot read my lips very well so Kent asked her for me and she said, "Yes".

Monday, December 13 *1982 – We had our first discussion with Betty Melvin this afternoon. Our missionaries from the 1st Ward, Elders Fontane and Yauncey, taught her. She seemed very eager and receptive to their message. She lives out by West Edmonton Mall and it is a very long way by bus so my Mom drove her home.*

Friday, December 24, 1982 *– My sister Kathy and Dad B came and picked up Albert, another patient at the Aberhart, and me, to go home for Christmas Eve. We had our big turkey dinner tonight. After dinner, we had our Christmas Eve Family Home Evening. Members of the family acted out the nativity while Dad B. read it out of our big Bible.*

Sunday, January 2, 1983 *– Today our meetings began at 9:00 a.m. and we just about made it on time. In testimony meeting, Dad, Mom, and I bore our testimonies. In my testimony I expressed my thankfulness for the power of the priesthood and for the blessing that my Dad B gave me after my stroke. Through that blessing, I was healed. The doctors told my Mom that the kind of stroke I had usually would take about a year to recover from and I was healed in less than a month. My sight returned almost immediately, and my speech is improving every day. I bore my testimony of the truthfulness of the gospel, that Jesus Christ is our Lord and Saviour and President Kimball is a prophet of God, as was Joseph Smith.*

Monday, January 3, 1983 *- Tonight, for Family Home Evening, we went bowling with the LeBaron family. Sister LeBaron and her daughter, Debbie, had never bowled five-pin bowling before. Debbie was getting upset with herself because she couldn't do it right. I told her to stop taking herself so seriously and to laugh at her mistakes. That's what I do.*

Jeannie Takahashi had been asked by the Stake Presidency, at the request of Elder Lorin C. Dunne, to write an article about Si for the New Era magazine. She phoned me several times for information and came one afternoon to spend a few hours with Si. I was really pleased that she had been asked to do this. She is a very talented person and lives close to the spirit. I knew she would do an excellent job and would write it as our Heavenly Father would want it done, to fulfill his purposes.

Tuesday, March 1, 1983 was the 8th anniversary of Si's accident. Marinus and I took Si to Institute class, as usual. After class I helped Si write in his journal about how thankful he was for the trials he had been called to bear, for the growth that he had received, and for the many things he had learned and accomplished that he felt he probably wouldn't have if he had all his physical capabilities. He has grown so very much spiritually and has such a strong testimony of the gospel. His knowledge of the gospel has grown tremendously as he has listened to the scriptures every day. He loves the Gospel and receives much joy from sharing it with others. He has given 20 copies of the Book of Mormon to people in the last few months and two ladies are taking the discussions. He is a living example to me that "true love casteth out all fear" because he isn't't afraid to talk to anyone about the Gospel. I am so proud of this wonderful son and so grateful to be his Mom.

Monday, April 9, 1982 – *Tonight we went to 9th Ward's Family Home Evening. Sheila Urban asked me to give the lesson in her group. I gave the lesson on the influence of music in our lives. I asked, first of all, what kind of music they liked to listen to. After we discussed that for a while, we played a tape by Boyd K. Packer called, "Worthy Music, Worthy Thoughts". It is a really good tape about the importance of listening to good music and disciplining our thoughts. He made the comparison of our thoughts to actors on a stage. He said there is always something playing on the stage of our minds and if it isn't something good, it will be something evil. He said that if something evil comes on our stage, we should think of a favourite hymn or scripture to replace the evil, because we cannot think of two things at once. Before we played the tape, my mom told a story from the New Era about music called "Apples or Onions". In it good music was compared to apples and poor music to onions.*

Thursday, April 12, 1984 – *My 26th birthday. Today I had a really great birthday. All the staff came in to wish me a happy birthday some time during the day. Quite a few of the staff came in with a birthday cake and sang Happy Birthday to me.*

This evening we had an Open House at our home for my birthday. People brought a lot of presents for me and I really appreciated this, but it wasn't necessary. My Mom took my journal home and people signed their names in it and many wrote little comments.

20

THE SI PETERSON AWARD

Color Night for students of the LDSSA (Latter Day Saint Student Association)
was held on Friday, February 13, 1986. During the program, they had the pre-
sentation of awards to students in the LDSSA for different things like sports and
academic achievements. This year a different award was presented. It was called
the "Si Peterson Award" and it was given to the LDSSA student who achieved
the most with what they had. This year it was awarded to Melanie Allen. About
2 ½ years ago, she was hit by a car on the way to Institute class. She was severely
injured. Her leg was broken in many places and she spent many months of suf-
fering in the hospital, but she was cheerful through it all.

Some of the requirements to receive this award are:

1. *Minimum university course load of 4 subjects.*

2. *80% attendance at Institute class.*

3. *Cheerfulness through trials and tribulations.*

When Sister Takahashi wrote the article about Si that was published
in the New Era in October of 1985, she received $150.00 for it. She
used this to purchase a plaque that was in the shape of the Province
of Alberta and had metal plates on it where names could be engraved.
At the top of the plaque was a picture of Si and the title "Si Peterson
Award". The criteria for receiving the award were printed on the back
of it. It would not necessarily be awarded every year.

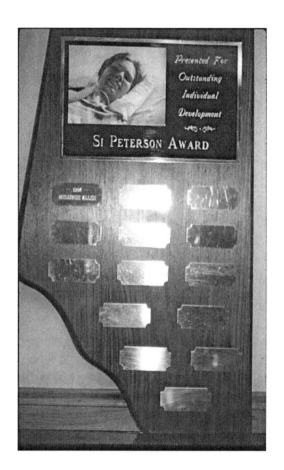

21

THE COMPUTER

One day a young man named Randy Bennett came to visit Si to talk to him about ways that he could possibly run a computer. He said that a lady named Elaine Heaton was giving a workshop at the Glenmore Rehabilitation Hospital about the different devices that handicapped people could use to run a computer. He left her phone number by Si's phone.

A few days went by and we both forgot about it. One morning, as I was returning home from doing my Visiting Teaching, the spirit said to me, "Go to Si's room and call Elaine Heaton now!" I have learned not to argue when these promptings come, so I turned around and went up to Si's room and phoned Elaine Heaton. The workshop she was giving was that afternoon and if I hadn't obeyed the spirit we would have missed it. This workshop opened our eyes to the wonderful opportunities that were available to help handicapped people, like Si, have a better quality of life.

Marinus went to a computer outlet and talked to a man named Seigfried Lipp who owned the store. He told Marinus that the needed equipment would cost about $8,500.00. He also told Marinus about the work the National Research Council in Ottawa was doing to help handicapped people run computers. Marinus phoned the National Research Council and talked to a man named Peter Nelson. He told Marinus that they had invented a mod keyboard and that he would like Si to be the first to try it out. We were really excited about this, but now we had the problem of how to afford to buy Si a computer, monitor, printer, etc.

One night I awoke and lay there trying to come up with solutions to this problem, when it suddenly came into my mind to have a "Si Peterson Computerama". This would be in the form of a program featuring all the best entertainers from the wards in Edmonton that would be willing to participate. I was so excited that I couldn't go back to sleep. I talked to Marinus about it and we decided to ask Eileen Hallett (Marinus' former wife) to direct it for us. I made an appointment with her to ask her to do this. She graciously accepted and, because she worked at Grant MacEwan College, she suggested that we use their auditorium for the production.

Several young men from the Single's Ward formed an orchestra to accompany the performers. Rhonda Goth helped Eileen with the production. We asked Jackie and Allen Champion to be the emcees. The entertainers were the Begieneman sisters (Marinus' four daughters), Kathy, Leslie, Renee and Monique who sang several numbers, Michael Murdoch who did several Elton John numbers, and Linda Purnell who accompanied Brother Murdoch and who also played a marvellous piano solo. We also showed "The Si Peterson Story" (Part II) that Bob Layton had put together.

The Computerama was held on October 13th and 14th, 1984. It was a great success! The auditorium was packed both nights and we cleared about $3,000.00.

The members of the 9th Ward (Single's Ward) with Brent Hatch as Bishop, decided to put on "Joseph and His Amazing Technicolor Dream Coat". They performed it for 5 nights and gave the proceeds to Si to help pay for his computer. They raised $2,500.00 and Bishop Hatch gave another $500.00, so now we had $6,000.00.

When Marinus went to purchase the computer, etc. for Si, the total came to $8,000.00. Seigfried Lip gave Si all the equipment he needed for the $6,000.00 and absorbed the remainder of the cost into his business. Another miracle had happened! How blessed we were!

The Research Council in Ottawa sent Si the Mod Keyboard. This was an interface that was put into the back of a Vic 20 computer. Two monitors were put on a table over Si's bed. One of them was connected to the mod keyboard and a computer keyboard appeared on the screen. The other was a computer monitor that Si worked on. He ran the computer with a TOSC (Touch Operated Systems Control). This was a device that sat in front of Si's mouth that he could touch with his lip to operate the computer. On the keyboard monitor there was a curser that went down the side of the keyboard and when Si wanted a letter on a certain row, he would touch the TOSC with his lip and the curser would go across that row, and then when he found the letter he wanted, he would touch the TOSC again and it would print the letter on his computer monitor. The cursor moved very, very slowly at first and Si would often miss the row that he needed, but he would just patiently wait for the cursor to go down to the bottom and back up again. He practiced and practiced so patiently for many hours every day.

About 2 weeks later, he asked me if the cursor could be made to go faster. I was amazed that he had mastered it so quickly. Marinus made it go quite a lot faster and Si was still able to run it. I told him he had the fastest lip in the west. After using it for several years, Si could type using his lip, almost as fast as people, who were not handicapped, could use their hands.

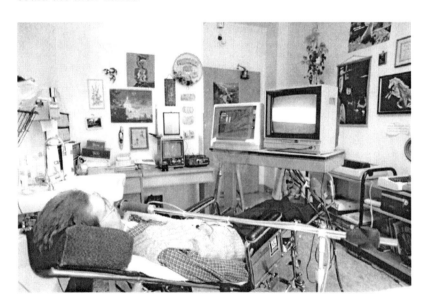

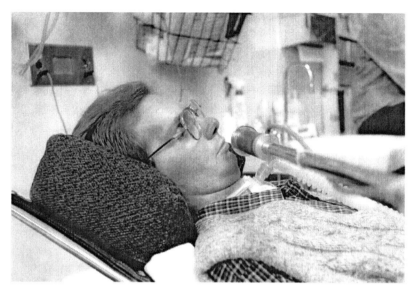

Marinus spent many hours teaching Si about computers and, through his patient tutelage, the computer became a great blessing in Si's life. Si said that when he used the computer, he didn't feel paralyzed at all.

Following is one of the wonderful articles that Si wrote using his computer.

The Bible and the Book of Mormon

There are several scriptures talking about the Book of Mormon in the Bible. I would like to share some of those scriptures with you and then as we study them and become more familiar with them, they will help us feel more confident as we endeavour to share the gospel of Jesus Christ and our testimonies of the Book of Mormon.

In Ezekiel 37:16-17 it says, "Moreover, thou son of man, take thee one stick, and write upon it, for Judah, and for the children of Israel his companions: then take another stick, and write upon it, for Joseph, the stick of Ephraim, and for all the house of Israel his companions: And join them one to another into one stick; and they shall become one in thine hand."

The stick of Judah is the Bible and the stick of Joseph is the Book of Mormon.

In the Book of Isaiah, Chapter 29, there are several references to the Book of Mormon. Elder LeGrand Richards explains the significance of these references very clearly in his book "A Marvellous Work and a Wonder". Isaiah saw the coming forth of the Book of Mormon as the voice of one that has a familiar spirit. It has a familiar spirit because, like the Bible, it contains the words of the prophets of God. The only way a dead people could speak out of the ground is through records that were buried in the earth.

Another scripture talking about the Book of Mormon is found in Psalms 85:11, "Truth shall spring forth out of the earth and righteousness shall look down from Heaven." We believe this is referring to the Book of Mormon because we believe the book is scripture from God our Father, also the plates the Book of Mormon was written on, were buried in the earth. Then in John 10:16, it says, "And other sheep I have which are not of this fold: them also I must bring, and they shall hear my voice; and there shall be one fold, and one shepherd." This scripture is talking about the people on the American Continent; some of them are the ancestors of the American Indians.

These scriptures have been preserved for us, in the dispensation of the fullness of times, to use as we go forth to flood the earth with the Book of Mormon. 1. Be an example of the truth in word and deed, 2. Share what we have been blessed with, with others, namely the Gospel of Jesus Christ as contained in the Bible and Book of Mormon, and we will be doing what the Lord commands, "When thou art converted, strengthen thy brethren." I believe this scripture is talking about our brothers and sisters both in and out of the church. We are required to do this until the great Jehovah shall say, "The work is done."

But before that can be accomplished, we must do as Nephi counsels, that is, "I will go and do the things which the Lord hath commanded, for I know that the Lord giveth no commandments unto the children of men, save he shall prepare a way for them that they may accomplish the thing which he commandeth them".

May we do these things and get out from under the condemnation we in the Church are under for treating lightly the Book of Mormon.

He could now keep his own journal, recording his feelings and thoughts without having to tell them to me so that I could record them for him. He also wrote articles for the 9th Ward bulletin, lessons for his home teaching people, and letters.

Shortly after he had mastered the computer, a power surge went through the hospital and, because we did not have a power surge protector on his computer, it wiped out all the things he had written. When I entered Si's room that afternoon, Si was lying with the curtains drawn and seemed really down. When he told me what had happened, I said a silent prayer to Heavenly Father that I would know what to say to comfort Si and lift his spirits up. I suddenly remembered something that had happened when Si was a little boy. He was about 2 ½ years old. His dad was in 3rd year Dentistry and it was the end of the university year. That whole year, Frank had been working on a project putting several dental procedures into a model of upper and lower teeth. He was to hand the finished project in that morning. The night before, he had left it on the kitchen table. Si got out of his bed early, went into the kitchen and thought this model was a wonderful toy and began clanging the upper and lower jaws together. All of the fillings, bridge-work and wonderful dental work that Frank had done on it were left in pieces on the table. His year's mark was based on this project and it was ruined. When Frank came into the kitchen and saw his year's work laying there in ruins, I was amazed at his reaction. He didn't say a word. He just went to the cupboard, got a paper bag, picked up all the pieces and put them in the bag, and left for the university. He worked all day and all night and redid the whole project. He got first class standing that year.

I told Si this story so that he could see the example that his Dad was to him in this event, and how he handled it with patience. As soon as I finished telling Si this story, he said, "Mom, could you please move my computer over and open the curtains. I'm ready to get to work again."

Whenever something happened to his computer and he couldn't work on it for a while, he said he felt like he was paralyzed all over again.

When Si moved to Regina with us in 1991, he was not able to take the TOSC with him because it belonged to the hospital. We were not sure what we were going to do, but then some friends came to the rescue again. Randy Marsden had a company called Madenta that made and distributed devices that helped handicapped people to live more meaningful and productive lives. When Randy was a university student, he and his friend Les Tann invented a device that they hoped would amplify Si's speech so that others could hear him. It never really worked, but we appreciated the thought and caring that went into it.

What Randy's company came up with, this time, was truly a miracle for Si. They provided Si with an Apple Computer and a very unique way for him to run it with the movement of his cheek. One of the employees of the company, Greg McGilles, came to Regina and set it all up for Si, and taught him how to use it. Our prayers had again been heard and answered!

Si enjoyed this new computer immensely, and learned to use it as proficiently as he had his other computer. We will be forever grateful to Randy for his kind generosity.

After Si passed away, Randy gave us a plaque that was inscribed with the following beautiful tribute to Si;

In Memory of Si Peterson
Whose Excitement For Life
Was The Inspiration For
Forming Madenta and To Whom
We Dedicate Our Future Endeavors
To Help All People
With Physical Disabilities

22
THE COACH

One Sunday, our Bishop asked if he could meet with Si. I wheeled Si into his office and, after chatting with him for a few minutes, Bishop Hudson called Si to be the coach of the First Ward's Softball Team. Si was a little stunned and wondered how he would be able to do that, but the Bishop assured him that he had every faith in him and knew he would do a good job.

Si loved to play ball before his accident, and was good at it, but he realized that coaching a team was a little different than playing so he was a bit apprehensive. I was thrilled with the calling and told Si that I would help him in any way that I could. Si accepted and became the coach of the First Ward's Softball Team.

I took Si to every game and practice, and because the members of the team couldn't read Si's lips very well, I would relay to them what Si had to say.

Si had this calling for a few years and thoroughly enjoyed it. The members of his team made him feel good about what he was doing. He said he often felt like the mascot of the team instead of the coach, but he enjoyed being part of a team again.

Lynn Merrell wrote the following letter to Si that helped him know that the calling that he had received to be the coach truly came from his Heavenly Father.

December 15, 1985

Dear Si,

I was thinking earlier today that I have never told you some-thing that may be personally important to you. When I was 1st Ward's physical activities director and presented your name to Bishop Hudson as the Ward's softball coach, I was not doing it just because I thought it would be a neat experience for you, but because the Lord had told me He wanted you to fulfill that calling. One Sunday afternoon, I was lying on my back on our living room rug pondering over who I could call to be the softball coach. I was quite concerned because I did not know who could do a good job, and just did not know whom to call. While I was pondering, you came into my mind, all of a sudden, like lightning. I lay there in amazement, because the answer was so easy, clear, and right. I thought, "Why didn't I think of that before!" My mind was full of light and I knew you were who Heavenly Father wanted to be the coach. I guess you know the rest. I thought this might be important to you, as it is to me. That experience reminds me often of God's love for us and that He inspires our leaders in calling the people He wants in a calling. I'm sorry I have waited so long to share this with you. Even though I do not say much to you Si, I want you to know I love you and you teach me so much that no other person in the world can teach me. I thank you for being the person you are. I hope you have a Merry Christmas.

Sincerely,
Lynn Merrell

23
THE TENTH ANNIVERSARY

March 1, 1985 - Today is the 10th anniversary of Si's accident. How quickly the time has passed. As I look back on it, it seems as if it was just a moment. We experienced many trials, in those 10 years, but we also received many blessings. I am sure that we would not and could not have grown as much without these trials in our lives. What a truly wonderful instrument Si had been in the Lord's hands, during these 10 years. As I visited with him today, I read some of the beautiful cards and letters that he had received from people over the years. I was amazed at the influence for good that he had been in the lives of so many people.

Jeannie Takahashi brought up a copy of the story she had written about Si for the New Era. I read it to Si and it was truly an inspiring article. The editors of the New Era had a hard time accepting the fact that Si had never railed against what had happened to him. It was hard for them to realize that he had accepted it completely as Heavenly Father's will and plan for his life. But after much deliberation they phoned Jeannie to say that they had decided to use the article in their magazine.

They sent a Brother McConkie to Edmonton to interview Si and to take some pictures for the article.

April 12, 1985 was Si's 27th Birthday. I would like to include in this chapter, an excerpt from my journal that I recorded that day.

"Today is my Si's 27th birthday. How very quickly time passes. It seems like only yesterday that I held that sweet new little baby in my arms. I shall never forget the great joy that filled my heart just knowing that he was really my very own baby and I could hold him and take care of him to my heart's desire. He was the fulfillment of a deep yearning and longing that had filled my very soul for a long time. How very grateful I am to my Heavenly Father for the gift of motherhood that he gave to me. What a sacred and overwhelming responsibility it is to be Si's mom. I don't know what I did in the Spirit World to have been given this privilege and responsibility but I am grateful for whatever it was, and for the trust my Heavenly Father has in me. Oh, how I pray that I will not let Him down. I have felt His presence so near to me, so many times, in these past 27 years, and I know that He is aware of my needs and weaknesses, and gives me strength when my courage lags and I become tired. I know that He will never give me more to bear than I can bear, with His help, and that I will always be made equal to the burdens that are placed upon me. This is a promise that I received in my Patriarchal Blessing, and I know that it is true."

On Sunday, September 22, 1985 a wonderful thing happened in Si's life. He was able to bless the Sacrament in 9th Ward's Sacrament Meeting. I was so grateful for Bishop Hatch and his counsellors, Bob Gilson and Michael Murdock, for the vision they had of what Si could do. They seemed to be able to think of things for Si to do that other people were afraid to suggest. How grateful I was for them.

Randy Ellis held the microphone for Si and he spoke into it. I'm not sure how well it was heard, but I know the spirit was really felt and everyone was moved by it.

The past two months had been really difficult ones for Si. He had experienced much pain and severe spasms. He had some kind of an infection in his lungs again, and he was losing a lot of weight. He only weighed about 90 pounds at the best of times, so he didn't have much reserve to go on. He looked very pale and sick and he had a large sore on his tailbone that was very, deep. In fact, the bone was protruding through his broken skin. Darlene, the head respiratory person, was very concerned about him as well. She said she would personally do some culturing of Si's sputum to see what germs he was growing. Marinus had given Si many blessings and I knew that that was what kept him going in spite of his illnesses. I also knew that the doctors would find what was wrong and would know how to help him.

24

THE NEW ERA ARTICLE

The article that Jeannie Takahashi wrote about Si was finally published In the October 1985 edition of the New Era. (LDS Church Youth Magazine). It was an excellent article and the pictures of Si, that they chose to use, were very good.

The article was entitled "A TYPICAL ONE-OF-A-KIND LATTER-DAY SAINT (to read it go to lds.org and click on Resources, click on Magazines, click on New Era, click on Other Issues, click on 1985, click on October 1985, click on A Typical One-of-a Kind Latter-day Saint)

It was also published in the International magazine — The Liahona. (to read it go to lds.org.Si Peterson Story)

Si received several letters from people, around the world, who read the article and were affected by it.

One day a friend of our family gave us the following story that had been printed in a magazine called "DE STER". It was written in Dutch and because my husband is Dutch, I thought he would be able to translate it for me. He tried, but found it too difficult. I did not know who to turn to for help in translating it. I even tried doing it myself, using a Dutch/English dictionary, but that didn't work either. I sent a copy to Holland with my husband when he went there to visit his gravely ill cousin, but did not hear back from the person he gave it to. I prayed hard that Heavenly Father would help me find someone that could translate it for me. On June 4th, 2010, my husband's sister and brother-in-law, who are both Dutch, came from Victoria for a visit. I mentioned to them that I was writing a book about Si and had it nearly done except for the translation of this story. They asked to see it and immediately told me that they could translate it easily because they both still read in the Dutch language. I was so grateful for them and that Heavenly Father had heard and answered my prayers.

Following is the article that was printed in De Ster followed by the translation that my husband's brother-in-law, Kees Boschma did for me:

Het begon in de bus

Erony Rosa A. Silva
ILLUSTRATOR SCOTT MOOY

In 1987 zag mijn oudste dochter Marcella twee jonge-mannen met naambordjes in de bus in Tiradentes (Brazilië) zitten. Ze raakten in gesprek en de zendelingen vroegen of ze meer over de kerk wilde weten.

Marcella had wel interesse, maar ze wist dat ik negatief over de heiligen der laatste dagen dacht. Ze zorgde ervoor dat ze bij een kerklid thuis les van de zendelingen kon krijgen, en uiteindelijk liet ze zich dopen. Ze was 19 jaar oud. Ik ging niet naar haar doopdienst omdat ik nog steeds radicaal tegen de kerk was.

In diezelfde tijd maakte ik een moeilijke periode in mijn leven door. Op zekere dag besloot ik om een paar tijdschriften door te lezen die ik nog had liggen. Daar zat ook een exemplaar van A Liahona (Portugees) bij. Ik vond het wel interessant.

In het exemplaar van februari/maart 1986 stond een artikel over Si Peterson, een jongeman uit Canada die verlamd was. Ik was vooral onder de indruk van het geloof en de volharding van zijn moeder.

In januari 1988 had mijn jongste dochter Monica een acute blindedarmontsteking en ze leed veel pijn. De arts zei dat ze onmiddellijk geopereerd moest woren. Marcella en ik brachten haar naar het ziekenhuis en probeerden haar zo goed mogelijk te troosten. In het ziekenhuis moest ik aan het verhaal denken dat ik in A Liahona had gelezen. Ik dacht vooral aan de moeder van Si, Anita Begienenman.

Marcella en ik hielden Monica stevig vast. We baden met al het geloof dat we hadden. Al snel merkten we dat ze weer wat kleur op haar wangen kreeg en ze hield op met huilen. Tot onze verbazing zei de arts dat er een vergissing in het spel was, en dat ze niet geopereerd hoefde te worden. Dankbaar en gelukkig gingen we alle drie naar huis.

Monica en ik besloten om de zendelingenlessen te volgen. We lieten ons op 19 maart 1988 dopen. Marcella is later in Zwitserland op zending geweest, en is nu getrouwd.

Door de voorbeelden van geloof in A Liahona ben ik tot de ontdekking gekomen dat mijn oude vooroordelen ten opzichte van de kerk niet juist waren. En ik heb er kracht uit geput in een moeilijke tijd. Vanaf die tijd is mijn getuigenis door middel van het tijdschrift voortdurend gesterkt. □

It Started In The Bus

In 1987 while riding a bus in Tiradentes, Brazil, my eldest daughter Marcella saw two young men with name tags sitting nearby. She started talking to the missionaries, and they asked her if she was interested in learning more about the church.

Marcella was interested, but she knew that I had negative feelings about the Mormon Church. She, however, took the discussions and was baptized at age 19.

I did not go to the baptismal service because I was still radically against the church.

During that same period, I went through some difficult times in my life.

One day I was leafing through some magazines that were lying around and came across a copy of a magazine called "The Liahona" that was written in Portugese, and I found it to be very interesting.

In the Feb. /Mar. 1986 copy was an article about Si Peterson, a young man from Canada who was paralyzed, and I was totally impressed by the faith and perseverance of his mother.

In January, 1988, my youngest daughter, Monica, had an acute appendicitis attack, and was suffering severe pain. The doctor told her that she needed an immediate operation. Marcella and I brought her to the hospital and tried, as much as possible, to comfort her.

At the hospital I thought again about the article I had read in the 'Liahona" and mostly, I thought about the mother of Si Peterson, Anita Begieneman.

Marcella and I held Monica tightly, and we prayed with all the belief we had.

Soon we noticed that some color was coming back to her face and she stopped crying.

To our amazement, the doctor told us that there had been a mistake and she did not need an operation. Thankfully, all three of us went home together.

Monica and I decided to take the discussions from the missionaries. We were baptized on March 19, 1988.

Later on, Marcella went on a mission to Switzerland and is now married.

Through the example of faith in the article I had read from the 'Liahona" I have come to the realization that my former thoughts about the Mormon Church were incorrect. I have received much faith from it in a very difficult time and my testimony has become stronger and stronger.

Translated by Kees Boschma

25

STRANGE FEELINGS

Si's PCO2 levels had been quite low for a few months. Low PCO2 can cause a condition called Alkalosis. Some of the symptoms of Alkalosis are: pain, weird sensations, hallucinations, and feelings of paranoia. Si had been experiencing all of these feelings for a few months, and we did not realize what was causing it. Si felt like he was being attached by evil spirits. This trial was almost more than he could bear, and we fasted and prayed that he would be given the strength and faith to stand it.

One day when Si was having a very hard time with these weird feelings, Marinus asked him if he would like another blessing. Si gratefully accepted. Marinus offered prayer and then laid his hands on Si's head and gave him the most beautiful blessing from his Heavenly Father. The spirit was so strong that I cried. In the blessing, Si was told that he was being prepared for Godhood, and that our Heavenly Father would not abandon him but would bless him and help him through every trial. He was told that in the councils of Heaven before he came to earth, he was given his life's mission. He knew that he would have an accident and be paralyzed, and he knew that it would be very hard but he accepted it and he would yet be very grateful for it. He was told that his Heavenly Father expected him to continue with his missionary work and to continue to work on his computer and to go to Expo and show others the great technical advancements that he had the privilege of using, so that other lives could be blessed. He was reminded of the great love that his Heavenly Father and his family had for him, and again was told that he would not be left alone.

It was a beautiful blessing of comfort, hope, and peace, and I knew that it came straight from our Heavenly Father.

After the blessing, Marinus expressed his great love for Si and bore testimony to him of the power of the Priesthood and the reality of our Saviour and his concern for each of us. How deeply grateful I was for the Priesthood that my husband held and exercised as he gave Si that beautiful blessing. My heart was so full.

One time when David was visiting with Si in our home in Lendrum, Si was experiencing feelings of being molested by evil spirits which troubled him greatly. David recounted the story to Si of Moses from the Pearl of Great Price (one of our books of scripture), where Moses commanded Satan, in the name of the Only Begotten of the Father, to depart from him, and Satan was compelled to leave. David reminded Si that he also held the priesthood and could command Satan to leave him when these feelings came. This was a great comfort to Si.

Si continued to be severely tested in many ways. He had severe pain that he said felt like his bones were melting, but he had such faith and was able to bear his suffering much better after receiving that beautiful blessing from Marinus, and found comfort through recalling the things that David had shared with him.

June 1, 1986 (an excerpt from my journal)

It is now almost midnight and the end of a beautiful Sabbath day. I attended meetings today with Si in the 9th Ward at the Institute building. Marinus helped me take Si there.

Yesterday Si wrote his testimony on his computer, printed it off, and I read it in testimony meeting today. It was a beautiful testimony and I have recorded it here

"Today, I would like to bear my testimony and thank Heavenly Father, Jesus Christ, the Holy Ghost, and all the faithful people who fasted and prayed for me. As you can see, it helped a lot. Things are still not back to normal, but they are a lot better. Physical pain was not the problem this time. There were mental and spiritual problems; and for me, those were harder to deal with than just mere pain, and I wish with every fibre of my being that it was over, but it is not and I don't think that it will be over until I die. I never wanted the Millennium to come as much as I do now, so I have been doing missionary work like never before. Many times I felt I couldn't go on, so I kind of gave up. Thank goodness there is repentance, so when I had straightened myself out and was ready to go on, I could do just that — go on. Almost everything the Holy Spirit tells me to

do, I do now, and you know what, the Holy Ghost is never wrong. He has been the greatest of all the great witnesses in the past and now.

I know that missionary work is the most important work to be engaged in next to the saving of our own souls. Our Saviour said, "This is my work and my glory to bring to pass the immortality and eternal life of man," but he cannot do it without our help.

I know that this is the true Church of Jesus Christ. I know that Joseph Smith was and is a prophet of God and I believe that he helps us with our missionary efforts. I am grateful for all the knowledge we have been given. I am grateful for all my many blessings, and I say this in the name of our Lord and Saviour, Jesus Christ, Amen."

What great happiness filled my soul as I read this beautiful testimony for my son.

26
EXPO 1986

Si was invited by the Neil Squire Foundation to go to Expo in Vancouver to demonstrate how he was able to run a computer.

We left Edmonton at 10:30 a.m. Friday, July 18th and drove to Kamloops, BC. We got there around 8:00 p.m. and stayed in a Travelodge motel. It had two double beds and was air-conditioned, so we had a very comfortable night. Si was quite short of breath while we were traveling, so I kept bagging him along the way, and then I put oxygen on him that night. The next day we kept the oxygen going while we traveled and we had a much better trip. We arrived in Vancouver around 5:00 p.m. and went directly to the place on the UBC campus where all the people involved with the Neil Squire Foundation were staying. We met a girl named Shayna who was Neil Squire's physiotherapist. She showed us where we were to stay in the Triumf House. We had a lovely room with a double bed and a sofa bed. It was all so clean and new. There was a communal kitchen with everything in it, where Marinus made Si's tube feeding and we were able to keep our food. The first night that Marinus made Si's tube feeding, there were several people in the kitchen and he got some very strange looks as he poured baby vegetables, baby meat, apple sauce, asparagus soup, and milk all in a bowl and mixed it up. I'm sure they thought he was going to drink it.

On Saturday evening, the Neil Squire Foundation had a lovely barbeque for all the people that had come to work in the special pavilion at Expo. It was held in front of the University housing where all the other people were staying. They had a short program and we were able to meet a lot of the people that Si worked with during the week. Richard, who had spent time in Edmonton helping Si with his computer, was there. It was good to see him again. He had been up in the Queen Charlotte Islands making a movie about the totem pole art made by the First Nation's People in that remote area.

After attending our meetings on Sunday, we went out to the pavilion at the Expo site to set up Si's equipment. It took a little longer than we had anticipated so Si was very tired when we returned and was having a very hard time breathing. Si's lungs were full of infection that I was sure was pseudomonas because of the terrible smell. I took a sputum sample in the night and Marinus took it to the hospital to be analyzed. Before we left Edmonton, Marinus gave Si and me each a blessing. Si was blessed that he would have good health and strength and be able to accomplish all that was required of him at Expo. This blessing was certainly fulfilled, because by Tuesday his lungs were totally cleared up, and he was comfortable without extra oxygen and was able to work at Expo for quite a few hours every day, without any discomfort, and enjoyed every minute of it.

I would like to tell you about my experiences at Expo. At the Expo site, I was placed in a big tent, sort of like a circus tent. It was called the Special Periods Pavilion and I worked there with 20 other handicapped people. I worked on the computer and people would gather around and Mom or Dad B. would explain what I was doing. I wanted to somehow share the gospel with those that stopped by, so I wrote down, on the computer, some things about myself — my name and where I came from, how my accident happened, and that I was a member of the Church of Jesus Christ of Latter-day Saints, sometimes known as the Mormon church. Many of the people when they found out that we were members of the church wanted to know more about it, so they asked a lot of questions. Some of the people that came around were members of the church and so we had some good conversations with them. One man that Mom and I talked to was a member of the church in Hawaii. He had about the same injury that I had. When his accident happened, he was told by the government and the hospital, that his life was over, but his wife and his mother fought the system and took him home to take care of him. They loved him too much to just let something like that happen because they knew the worth of his soul in the Lord's eyes and acted upon it.

(When Marinus and I visited Hawaii in 1988, we were able to meet with this wonderful man and his wife and renew our friendship with them.)

Monday evening we went to a special reception in BC Place on the Expo site where we met some of the Expo officials and the Mayor of Vancouver. It was a lovely evening. Si was a bit dizzy during the evening, so Bill Cameron put a case of beer under his wheels to tip him back, and everyone got a kick out of that because everyone knows that Si is a good Mormon and doesn't drink alcoholic beverages.

On Wednesday evening, Si, Marinus, and I had supper with Bill and Peggy Cameron at the UBC Faculty Club. They talked about Neil Squire and told us about his accident, his life, and his death. He was a 20-year-old UBC student when his accident happened in 1980. His car hit some black ice and slid into some trees. His spinal cord was severed, and he was paralyzed from his chin down. He lived for 4 years and then lost his life because of an undetected bleeding ulcer. He was a brave and valiant young man and was an influence for good in the lives of many people. The Neil Squire Foundation was named after him. It was dedicated to helping handicapped people have a better quality of life.

On Friday, the last day Si worked at Expo, Neil Squire's mom and sister visited the pavilion where Si and the others were working. Neil's mom saw Si in his too small chair and offered to give him Neil's chair. Neil had purchased a beautiful $15,000 computerized electric wheelchair a few months before he died and it was being stored in his mother's basement. We were so grateful and excited about this offer. Before we went home, we drove to Nanaimo and picked up the chair.

After church the following Sunday, we went to the apartment on False Creek where handicapped young men lived. Katrina, from the Neil Squire Foundation, took us there. It was such a beautiful place and I wished that Si could live in a complex like that. The six young men who lived there were all high Quads like Si but they all sat up straight in their chairs, talked out loud, ate with their mouths, and turned their own heads, things that Si was not able to do. We learned so much while we were there. They were breathing on 1800 - 2000 ccs of air or at least their volumes were set that high. They actually breathed on about 800 ccs and talked with the rest.

When we got home from Expo, we tried this with Si and he was able to talk a little, too. How I wished that we had known about all of this years before. Si also tried to strengthen his neck muscles but it had been too long since they had been used.

After visiting at the handicapped housing, we went to a little get — together at one of the units where some of the people stayed who worked at Expo. It was July 27th, Marinus' 50th birthday. They presented him with a beautiful birthday cake and sang Happy Birthday to him. The Cameron's, their daughter Suzie, Shayna, Katrina, Cyril, and many handicapped friends that Si had met during the week were there. It was a wonderful get-together and it was really hard to say goodbye to them at the end of it. After we got home, we received letters from Shayna, Katrina, and the Camerons.

During that last evening together, they played a tape of the Neil Squire theme song that a fellow named Brian Tate had written. It is called, "I Have a Voice".

It was so beautiful that there wasn't a dry eye in the room after we listened to it. Shayna gave us a copy of it and I played it at the fireside that Si and I did, about his trip to Expo, for the 9th Ward in Edmonton.

I HAVE A VOICE

When I'm all alone,
And it feels like there's nothing I can do,
I remind myself that yesterday
Can lead to something new
And I open up my eyes.
When I do something for myself,
I get a glimpse of freedom.
When I reach out to someone else
I feel that I could fly.
I can paint for you a picture,
I can write for you a song,
Such a new experience,
Now I know that I belong.

Chorus

I have a voice to be heard,
Line by line, word by word,
Let me tell you how I feel,
Let me show you who I am.
I have a dream — it's alive,
I can live — not just survive.
Watch me grow — set me free,
Cause I know what I can be.
It's my choice,

I HAVE A VOICE!

Day after day,
I think of trying to face the world alone,
But I know inside
That no one has to make it on their own,
And I open up my heart.
And when I feel I can't go wrong,
I feel a force inside me saying…
"Hold on to your dreams
'Cause you don't harbour excuses anymore!"
Just to say, 'I love you!',
That's a miracle to me.
Just to feel alive again
What a feeling that can be.

Chorus

So much of life I've yet to live,
I've had my share of joy and sorrow,
I know I've got so much to give.
It's time to move,
Move on to tomorrow!
I can paint for you a picture,
I can write for you a song,

Such a new experience,
Now I know that I belong.

Chorus

On Monday, July 28th, we left for Vancouver Island. We traveled over on the ferry and Si enjoyed this new experience. When we arrived at the home of Marinus' sister, Rea Boschma, she and her husband Kees had set up a hospital bed in the basement for Si. It was so easy for us to get him in there and we were so appreciative of their thoughtful kindness.

On Tuesday, we took Si to the Butchart Gardens with Oma Begieneman. (Marinus' mother) It was so beautiful there. We stayed for the show in the evening and also watched the dancing fountains. Marinus pushed Si, and I pushed Mom in a wheelchair, too, because it was a very long way to walk.

On Wednesday, we drove to Nanaimo, to the Squire home, and picked up Neil's chair for Si. They were such wonderful people and treated us so graciously.

The chair was beautiful and, with a few minor adjustments, fit Si really well. He and Neil were approximately the same size. We couldn't tip him back in it when he got dizzy because it was too heavy but, by accident, we learned that raising Si's arm caused his blood pressure to increase and the dizziness would go away.

It was quite late when we got back to Kees and Ria's and Si was very tired. Those bad feelings started bothering him again, so Marinus gave him a blessing. Si had such faith and felt better as soon as the blessing was finished. As Marinus and I attended the temple in December, Marinus was told, by the Spirit, that the trials that Si was experiencing were for his growth. They were necessary.

I was so grateful for this knowledge, and although the trials were still there, it helped Si and us to know that there was a reason and specific purpose for them. We continued to pray that he would receive the strength necessary to endure and learn from them.

On the way home, we stopped at the Shawnessy hospital in Vancouver, and Shayna and some other people who knew how to run Neil's chair, met us there and showed us how the chair worked

It was quite a complicated mechanism, but Si was able to run it for a little ways in the hospital. It was run by manoeuvring a control with his mouth.

The computer system in the chair broke a few days after we got home and we had to send to Ohio for a new part. When the chair was repaired, Si had a wonderful time practicing running it in the hallway of the Aberhart and scaring all the nurses with it. He also enjoyed using it at church where he could get himself around without having someone push him.

Shortly after we arrived home from Expo, Si was asked to speak at a fireside on the subject "Understanding the Handicapped and How to Fulfill Their Spiritual and Temporal Needs. Si wrote it out on his computer and I delivered it for him.

"I am grateful for the opportunity that I have had to prepare this talk for you. The topic that I have been asked to address is: UNDERSTANDING THE HANDICAPPED AND HOW TO FULLFIL THEIR SPIRITUAL AND TEMPORAL NEEDS.

I feel that it is really hard to fully understand a handicapped person unless you have that same handicap. Because I was sixteen when my accident happened, I remember what it is like in both situations and so I understand how hard it must be for some of you to know what to say or do for me. As I thought about this I feel the best way to understand the handicapped is to get to know them.

You know I wish that all of us had the openness of little children. When they meet me for the first time, they come right out and ask me what happened to me. They aren't afraid or embarrassed or afraid of embarrassing me, and I think that is really great and I wish everyone would do that.

Because there are some of you here who don't know that much about me, and are probably afraid to ask, I'll tell about myself. I am a quadriplegic. That means that I am unable to use any of my four limbs. I am totally paralyzed from my chin down. I cannot breathe at all on my own and so a respirator breathes for me, and because no air comes over my vocal chords, I cannot talk out loud. I can hear, however, and can communicate with you if you have the time and patience to read my lips. I can't swallow very well so I am not able to eat with my mouth very often. My food is poured down a tube directly into my stomach. I do not have the sense of smell and I cannot even turn my own head. I used to

*think that it would be a lot harder being a paraplegic because they are more able
to do the things they used to do so greater expectations are placed upon them.
Because I am so totally handicapped, no one really expected me to do anything,
and if I did anything everyone thought it was really great. But now, with the
advent of computers for the handicapped, many things are possible even for me
in the working world. Since I got my computer my world has really opened up
and I am so grateful for it. Whenever it isn't working, I feel like I'm paralyzed
all over again.*

*I think the most important need that I or any handicapped person has is
to be accepted — to be treated like a normal person. The only real difference
between you and me is that you have a body that works and I don't, but I am
still the same person inside this body that I was before my accident. I need you to
look beyond my chair and my still body to the person that is me, and realize that
I do have something to contribute and then take the time to find out what that
is. I think the Neil Squire Foundation theme song expresses what I am trying to
say and I would like to share the words of it with you*

*I would also like to share with you a quote from a lady named May Dang.
She is also a member of the Neil Squire Foundation. May suffers from Lou
Gering's disease, and is unable to walk or talk out loud.*

*"Whether healthy or not, we all march to the tune of a different drummer.
There is definitely a stigma attached to being non-verbal. People automatically
think one is deaf, dumb, and mute. Although it is not intentional on their part,
they speak loudly and enunciate words dramatically in the hope that I can lip
read. Sometimes people will spell words out on my word board.*

*Not being able to speak, one facet of my personality — my wit and humour,
remain anonymous. Telling a joke on an alphabet board loses all its oomph.*

*I look forward to the day when the shackles and chains are unlocked from my
throat, my arms and my legs, and in God's eyes I will be able to stand up and be
counted as a productive and useful person once again."*

*I feel that she has expressed, well, how many handicapped people feel, but
I disagree with some of her comments. I feel that as members of the church we
should all march to the beat of the same drummer whether we are handicapped
or not, and that drummer is our Saviour Jesus Christ. If we don't, we may
find ourselves in trouble we can't handle. Also I feel bad that she does not see
herself as a productive and useful person in her Heavenly Father's eyes. Every
person upon the earth, no matter what condition they are in, is of worth to our*

Heavenly Father and should try to do their best regardless of the condition in which they must spend their life.

I really empathize with her comment that, because she cannot talk out loud, some people automatically think she is deaf and dumb. It does help to have a sense of humour because being a quad does have its humorous moments.

People will ask my Mom to ask me how I am and when my Mom tells them to ask me, they say, "Oh, does he know how to read lips?"

When Mom takes me shopping it is really funny to watch people trying to look at me without appearing to stare. They often run into other people or trip over things as they look out of the corner of their eyes at me and can't watch where they are going. Some people think I am a girl and ask my Mom, "Whatever happened to 'her', and then my Mom has to explain my condition to them without saying "he" so that she doesn't embarrass them.

I remember one time when I was shopping with my favourite orderly and as we sat in the mall watching people go by, some would stop and ask Bob what happened to me. He would tell a different story every time like, "Oh he was skydiving and his parachute didn't open," or "He was on drugs and this is what happened to him." I'm sure the people were wondering why I was laughing so hard or trying hard not to laugh.

Most of my physical needs are taken care of by the nursing staff at the Aberhart Hospital or by my parents when I am home, but I sometimes feel, especially when I am in the hospital, that I am a patient first and a person second. Handicapped people need to be seen as a person first and this is where you, our brothers and sisters in the gospel, can help so much by taking the time to get to know us. Please don't be afraid! We are just ordinary people who are trapped inside bodies that don't work exactly right. Many of you are already doing this and I appreciate it very much. I would especially like to thank Mark Hume for being here every Sunday to sit by me in Priesthood meeting. He has become my really good friend.

If you have a handicapped friend that has to spend a lot of time in an institution or shut-in at home, the best way you can meet their needs is to visit them, (hint, hint). Remember that Jesus commanded us to visit the sick, and through King Benjamin He said, "When ye are in the service of your fellowmen, ye are only in the service of your God." Also in Matthew He said, "Inasmuch as ye have done it unto one of the least of these my brethren, ye have done it unto me." Isn't that great to know that when we do something for someone, like visiting *them, it is like we are doing it for our Heavenly Father, so what a privilege it should be!*

I feel that one of the best ways that the spiritual as well as the temporal needs of an individual can be fulfilled is through the Home Teaching and Visiting Teaching programs of the church. I am so grateful for the Home Teachers that have been assigned to me. Brother Beaumier and Brother Herrick are really great men and they have done so much for me. Whenever I am sick and cannot attend my meetings, they come and bring me the Sacrament. They take the time to talk to me to find out if there is anything bothering me and what my needs are at the time. Many times they give me blessings when I have a special need. It is great to know that they are there and I can call on them whenever I need to. They make me feel important and I know they really care about me.

I am also very thankful for the help and strength I receive daily from my Heavenly Father. He has really blessed me and I know He will never give me more to bear than I can bear, with His help. I receive the greatest spiritual strength from the example that my Saviour is to me. Whenever I start feeling sorry for myself, I think of all He suffered and went through for me, and I realize that he understands every pain or trial or problem that I could possibly have. He was persecuted, spit upon, ridiculed, whipped, put on a cross, nailed to it with big spikes, and left to hang until He died. And typical of His greatness, He made this most loving statement just before he died, "Father forgive them for they know not what they do." I know my Saviour lives and loves me, as does my Heavenly Father. I know that I belong to the true Church and that it contains the fullness of the Gospel of Jesus Christ. I'm proud to be a member of it and I bear this witness in the name of Jesus Christ amen".

27

THE PATCH AND THE HOLE

On February 4, 1987 we took Si to the new University of Alberta Hospital to Station 5D3 so that surgery could be done on his tailbone. He had a sore there that would not heal. The operation was successful. They took skin and tissue from his buttocks and attached it to his tailbone. It looked like a big patch. They also stitched-up the other big sore that he had on his bottom.

There was a young man named Larry Lightning in the next bed to Si. He had a car accident in the fall of 1986 and became a paraplegic. He had quite a lot of feeling return, and was being weaned from the respirator. He could move his arms and was getting some feeling back in his legs. I visited with him while the nurses were busy with Si. Larry had had the same operation on his bedsores that Si had.

On February 19th, Si went back to the Aberhart. He was glad to be back 'home'. They started getting him up for short periods — about 10 to 15 minutes each day. Si's sores continued to heal well, and he was soon able to get up in his chair for longer periods of time.

On March 9th, Barb and I got up really early to prepare to leave for Toronto to visit with Leigh Ann and Eric. Marinus took our suitcases to the airport and picked up our tickets.

The phone rang about 8:00 a.m. It was Maureen McQuaid, a nurse from the hospital. She said that both of Si's lungs had collapsed and they were taking him to the ICU. I hurried and got ready as fast as I could and arrived there just after he got there.

Si had been having a very hard time breathing lately and was very short of breath most of the time. His lungs just seemed to constantly have infections and he had several bouts of pneumonia. His lungs were weakened by all the infections. When they turned him onto his back to give him a chest x-ray, he had a severe spasm that blew a hole in one of his lungs. The air then escaped into the plural cavity and collapsed both of his lungs. He was in very serious trouble for a few minutes, but again our Heavenly Father knew this was going to happen and had help there immediately. Dr. York and Darlene, the respiratory nurse, had just arrived on Station 81 and were able to attend to him immediately. He went under a bit, but they got hoses in his lungs quickly and he revived. How grateful I was for Heavenly Father's protection of Si. I don't know what I would have done without this assurance and faith in Him.

When I entered Si's room in the ICU, his face was all swollen up from the air going into his tissues when they bagged him. He looked like a 300 pound man. It really frightened me until the doctor explained what had happened and said that it would go away. Si was still quite short of breath, but they could not bag him. He was on a large respirator and I think it breathed differently for him than his own respirator did. My heart went out to him. I felt so helpless not being able to help his body get all the air it needed.

Marinus arrived and gave Si a blessing. It really helped him. I then had a hard decision to make and, even as I stood there struggling; I knew what I would do. I wanted so very, very much to go to Toronto to see my Leigh Ann and Eric, but I knew that Si needed me too, and I needed to be there with him through this latest trial. Si said that I should go and that he would be all right, but I thought of how I would feel if I was Si — would I want my Mom to leave me? Without any hesitation, the answer came. I decided to stay. Barbie was a little upset because I think she was afraid to fly there alone, but I knew that she would be all right and that she and Leigh Ann would have a good time together. I also knew that Leigh Ann would understand why I hadn't come.

On March 11th, Si was able to be moved back to the Aberhart. I went with him in the ambulance. His breathing was much easier and he was in good spirits.

A few days later, Si got a badly infected wisdom tooth. They give him some antibiotics to take away the infection. Si was also having major problems with his heart racing and shortness of breath. As I sat by him, I noticed that every time he was tube- fed, his stomach or abdomen would go into a hard ball and then his heart would start to race and he would get very short of breath. I told this to the doctor and he said that Si was 'dumping'.

Dumping happens in people who have serious surgery on their stomachs for ulcers. Instead of staying in the stomach for a while, Si's tube feeding was moving directly into his intestines and this caused extreme pain. Although Si could not feel the pain, his body could, and it reacted by causing his heart to pound and his stomach and abdomen to spasm into a hard ball. To alleviate this problem, they began letting his tube feeding drip into his stomach very slowly from a bag attached to an IV pole. This worked really well, and his breathing became much easier.

On April 5th, we attended both satellite sessions of LDS Church General conference at the stake center. Si was able to attend with us. He also went to the Priesthood session on Saturday evening. When we got back to the hospital, Marinus gave Si a Priesthood blessing. It was a most wonderful blessing that I knew would help Si's life. I wish that I had total recall so that I could remember everything that he was promised, but the one thing that stands out most in my mind is that he was blessed that he would be married and have children who would love and honour him. He was also blessed that he would be able to overcome the evil influences that were around him. He was told that he was a valiant spirit, and that he would stand with the noble and great ones in the spirit world.

28

HOUSING

When we returned from Expo in 1986, I told the people who lived at the Aberhart about the wonderful housing for handicapped people that we had visited at False Creek in Vancouver. We immediately began looking into the possibility of having something similar built in Edmonton. After doing much research about location and cost, etc., we arranged a meeting with some Government officials to present our findings and to petition for funding. I made a video that was presented at the meeting because I was unable to be there.

The following statement is what I said on the video.

"I am sorry that I am unable to be at your meeting in person, but I am grateful for the opportunity to speak with you on video. My name is Anita Begieneman and I am the mother of Si Peterson. Twelve years ago, Si fell from a high bar in a school gymnasium and broke his neck at the first cervical level. His spine was severed and he became instantly and totally paralyzed from his chin down. He is unable to breathe on his own at all, so is 100% respirator dependent. He cannot even turn his own head; but from his chin up, he is very normal and is a bright young man with a great sense of humour.

Si spent five months in the Intensive Care Unit at the University Hospital and then was transferred to the Aberhart where he has resided ever since. Although Si is extremely handicapped physically, his mind is bright and alert, and he has maintained a very positive mental outlook through the years. He has continued his education with the help of correspondence courses and tutors. He has coached a softball team for three years and he attends church and other functions each week and is home most weekends.

During the twelve years that Si has been a patient-resident at the Aberhart, he has received excellent care, but because it is a hospital, I feel that his physical needs take precedence over all the other needs that he has as a person. It seems that he is a quadriplegic first and a person second. It is sometimes hard for the nursing staff to remember that he is more than a trach, a g-tube, or a catheter.

We, his family and his friends, have always tried to meet his other needs, but we have always hoped and wished that someday he would be able to live more independently and out of an institutional setting.

About three years ago, Si was able to acquire an IBM PC. This has really opened up his life in many ways. Last summer, he was invited to go to Expo and demonstrate how he uses his computer. It was there, while we were in Vancouver, that we had the opportunity to visit the residence for high quads on False Creek called Creekview 202. What a revelation this was to us. We did not even know there were six other high level quads, like Si, in Canada. We were certainly surprised to see them living in an independent housing situation and enjoying such a quality of life outside of an institutional setting. We were very impressed with this.

I will not go into the structural or organizational details of this complex because that will be on the video, but I was very impressed with the relaxed, happy atmosphere I felt there. We were able to visit with five of the six residents of Creekview that day, and they all expressed how much they enjoyed living there. One thing they all mentioned was that they had been free of the chronic respiratory infections that seem to plague patients living in an institutional setting. In the year they had been there, not one of them had to be hospitalized. The physical part of their person had become secondary.

When we returned from Vancouver, we were so excited and full of hope that, if this type of independent living was possible for these six men, it certainly was possible for Si.

We immediately, upon our return from Expo, contacted the American Paraplegic Association to see what handicapped housing was available. We then visited every unit in the city and attended a meeting with those involved with Abbey Road Housing. After meeting with residential aids people, respiratory technicians, and social workers, we realized that none of these units were suitable for a respirator-dependent individual. We realized that a place similar to Creekview was the only solution. We didn't know where to turn for help, and then, about ten days later, Mrs. Payne informed me about a letter she had received from you, and I felt that perhaps, at last, our prayers were being answered and that a brighter, more independent future might be possible for Si and others like him. On behalf of all these people, I thank you for listening to me today, and I hope that you will consider our project to be worthy of your funding assistance."

This housing did get built, and one day a woman phoned to ask me if Si would be interested in moving there, and if so, how many hours he would require a caregiver each day. I told her that he required 24 hour care because he could not breathe on his own. She again asked, "But how many hours does he actually need someone there?" I again told her that he required 24 hour care. She was quiet for a moment and then said, "Oh, I'm afraid that would not be possible."

I was so disappointed. Somehow the whole concept of an independent living place for handicapped people, like the one on False Creek in Vancouver, had been lost. This, again, would not be a suitable place for Si and others like him. The Aberhart Hospital would remain 'his home away from home'.

29

THE HOLIDAY MIRACLE

In July 1990, Marinus and I spent a week on a little vacation. When we returned, we went up to the Aberhart to get Si ready for his holiday. When we got there, the nurse informed us that Si was critically ill, and there was no way that he could ever go on a holiday. She said that his intestines and bowels had stopped working, and he was being fed a substance called Criticare. He was being given 30 ccs of it every hour. She said that usually people on Criticare only live for about 3 months. She told me all this with tears in her eyes. I was very upset. I went to Marinus, who was in the wheelchair room getting Si's chair ready. I told him what the nurse had said and asked him to give Si a blessing. I called Ben to come and assist Marinus with the blessing. He came and Ben anointed Si, and Marinus gave him a most beautiful blessing. He was blessed that his health would be restored, that his body would function properly, that his time to leave this earth was not yet, that he had a great work to do upon the earth, and that all would be well on his holiday.

With my faith and courage restored, I asked the nurse to get Dr. York on the phone for me. She did and I told Dr. York that we wanted to take Si on his holiday. He also told me how very ill Si was and that they could not recommend that he leave the hospital. I told him that I felt it was very important that Si go on a holiday to see his grandma in Victoria and that we would take full responsibility for him.

Dr. York arrived at the hospital a short time later and gave me several papers to sign, releasing the hospital of all responsibility for our decision. I asked him what I could feed Si by mouth, and he said that I should not give him anything but Criticare food through his

G-tube. I then said that I wanted to give him something by mouth and asked him again for his advice, and he said that I could probably give him some pudding or yogurt. He said that he wished with all his heart that he could give us his blessing in what we were doing, but he just couldn't. I appreciated his concern, but knew that Si would be all right. How I wish that everyone in the world were members of our church and believed as we do, so that we could tell them about priest-hood blessings.

We left with Si early Tuesday, July 3rd, and travelled to Kamloops that day. Si had to have his Criticare every hour and 18 different medicines or supplements given at different times. It kept me on my toes, so that I didn't miss any, and it was quite a challenge trying to get it into his G-tube syringe without spilling any as we travelled on the bumpy roads. It seemed like every time I would go to pour it in, Marinus would go over a bump. Si and I had some good laughs over it.

Si was so happy to be going. It was worth every effort just to see the beautiful smile on his face and to bring a little change and excitement into his life.

When we got to Kamloops, we bought some pudding and yogurt, and he really enjoyed eating them.

We had a good night, a good trip the next day, and arrived in Victoria on Wednesday evening. Ria had a hospital bed for Si in the basement bedroom and everything was fixed up so nicely for us.

That night I did Si's bowel routine. His bowels had not moved at all for quite some time while he was in the hospital, so I wasn't sure what to expect. Well, I got more than I expected! About 3:00 a.m., I got up to turn Si and to check on his bowels, and he had done a bowel movement like I had never seen before. It was really runny and very dark in color and filled two large lap pads. I could hardly believe what I was seeing. My heart was so full of thankfulness that his body pro-cesses were beginning to function properly again. I felt like dancing all over the room with joy. I had to smile to myself that something like a bowel movement could cause me such happiness. I'm sure if anyone could have seen me they would have thought that I wasn't quite right in the head.

Si's face had quite a few very bad pimples on it, so I gave him a complete facial every day and the change in his complexion was truly amazing.

We spent a lot of time with Grandma Begieneman in her beautiful retirement home. We took her for a long drive up the Malahat and had lunch at the Malahat Café.

Si's health improved each day. We stayed in a little town near Kamloops on our way home on Saturday night. I did Si's bowel routine again, and it was perfectly normal. His stomach was flat, his lungs were very clear. I only had to do instillations every other day, and his complexion was beautiful. A real healing had taken place in his body, as had been promised in the blessing.

We continued on our drive home early Sunday morning. We stopped along the way and had a little church service. After it was over, Marinus gave Si another beautiful blessing and then a wonderful thing happened. Si asked if he could give Marinus a blessing. This was such a tender and special event as Si's hands were placed on Marinus's head and Si pronounced a beautiful blessing of comfort and hope upon him. I shall cherish this always in my memory.

We arrived home quite late Sunday evening, so we decided to keep Si home and take him back the next day, so the doctors and nurses could see how very well he was. To say that they were amazed and surprised would be an understatement. They just could not believe the change. Si exuded good health. His face shone, and his eyes were bright and alert. Our prayers and the blessing Si had received had truly been answered. A male nurse asked if he could talk to me. He told me that when I had insisted on taking Si on his holiday against doctor's orders, the staff had really resented me and thought I was acting irresponsibly, but when they saw the results, they changed their attitude and gave me credit. I told him that it had very little to do with me. Si had been healed because of prayer and faith.

I asked Dr. York if Si could be given normal food blended into tube feeding instead of Osmolite that he was being given, and he said that they would try it. Si's health stayed quite good except for a lung infection that appeared again. They put him back into isolation because of a staph infection around his G-tube.

30

THE ROLL OVER

Si's youngest sister, Barbara was married to Richard Steele in the Idaho Falls Temple on August 19, 1990. After the wedding a small family reception was held for them in the Shilo Inn. After the reception, Barb and Rich left on their honeymoon, and Marinus, Si, Lori and her three children (Stacey - 10, Lindsay - 3 and Breanne - 1) and I drove to Helena, Montana and spent the night there. When we got to our motel room we ordered pizza and crazy bread and had a little party. We finally went to sleep around midnight.

Si had a fairly good night. We awoke early Sunday morning and were on our way home again by 9:00 a.m. Usually when we travel on Sunday, we stop somewhere and have our own little church service, but Marinus was anxious to get home. We had a long way to go and he had to work the next day, so we just listened to hymns and kept traveling.

Marinus was driving and, a little after noon, he became very sleepy. He pulled over and asked if Lori or I could drive for a while. I told him no because I had been up with Si quite often in the night and I knew I just couldn't stay awake. Lori also said she was very sleepy because she had been up with her baby in the night, but she said she would give it a try. I told her to stop if she got the slightest bit sleepy, and she said she would.

About an hour later, I got up to move Si in his chair so that he wouldn't get any sores. After I had positioned him, I thought that I wouldn't do up his top seatbelt because it looked uncomfortable to me. But the spirit said to me, "Do up both seatbelts!" I argued for a minute, but then decided to obey. I did them both up and had just settled back into my seat beside Si, when I felt the van go into the rough on the left side of the road. The next thing I knew we were across the road and going into the ditch on the right side. I jumped up and put my arms around Si to protect him just as the van flipped up onto its roof and then rolled 2 or 3 times. I was thrown over Si, and my back hit the lift. Stacey was not belted either, so she was also rolling around. The thought that crossed my mind was that I felt like clothes in a clothes dryer. The van finally came to rest on its wheels with the motor still running. Stacey and I were on the floor behind Si's chair. Si's head was hanging off his headrest, and it was bleeding very badly. His blood was running down all over me. I tried to reach up to put his head back on the headrest, but my back was hurting so badly, I couldn't reach it. Si's respirator alarm was ringing. His battery had flown off his chair and his hosing was all apart. He was not breathing! Lori, who we found out later had a cracked vertebrae in her neck, climbed over Si's legs and blew in his trach hole until Marinus was able to get everything back together again. Marinus had a bad cut over his right eye. Si's head was cut in several places. His teeth were all knocked sideways, and he had a bad cut over his right eye as well. I suffered a serious injury to my lower back. We found out later that the extreme pain I felt was because my L1 vertebra was shattered. The little ones, Breanne and Lindsay, were fine. Amazingly, they didn't even cry. We were all alive! A miracle had occurred!

There was an empty ambulance coming down the road on the other side when this all happened. He came across the median and was there by the time the van stopped rolling. The van roof was very smashed in, but the side where the lift was, was all right, so that the lift still worked. They got Si out of the van and into the ambulance very quickly. The paramedic had phoned for other ambulances, and they arrived shortly. He told us later that when he saw the accident happen, he thought to himself, "There will be no one alive in that van!"

The first person on the scene was a Dr. Palmer from Calgary. He reached through the back doors and pulled me up onto the back seat. When Marinus finished helping Si, he turned to the people that had gathered and asked if anyone held the Melchezidek Priesthood. Brother Palmer said, "I do", so Marinus asked him to assist in giving me a blessing. Marinus gave me a blessing of comfort and healing.

The paramedics strapped me to a board and lifted me out of the back doors of the van. We were taken by ambulance to Conrad, Montana, where Marinus' and Si's cuts were stitched. But they couldn't do anything for Lori and me there so we were taken by ambulance to Great Falls.

Marinus called Brian (Lori's husband), and he and his two brothers, Wayne and Kendan, came in a van and brought Si and Marinus to Great Falls. A bishop in one of the wards in Great Falls found a motel for Marinus and Si to stay in. Marinus stayed with Si. In the night, Si suddenly became very upset, and Marinus was not able to settle him down. He took him to the Great Falls hospital emergency department where Marinus took care of him for three hours because the people there didn't know what to do for him. They finally did a CT scan on him, but they couldn't find anything wrong.

The next morning, Marinus phoned Barb Schmidt, the charge nurse at the Aberhart Hospital, to tell her what had happened. She and a respiratory technician came on a Lear jet and took Si to the University Hospital in Edmonton. Si spent 10 days in the ICU, not really knowing where he was, or who he was, or what had happened. His stepmother, Jen, and a friend, Dawn Norwood, were there to meet the jet when it came in. I was so relieved when I was told that Si had been flown back to Edmonton. What a very scary and exhausting experience my husband went through in trying to care for Si and worry about me, too!

Lori and I were in the same room in the Great Falls Hospital. I was given some kind of drug that took the pain totally away and left my mind very clear. A nurse at the hospital was originally from Raymond, Alberta so she called my brother-in-law's sister, Della Helgerson-Johnson, who lived in Great Falls, and told her we were there. She came several times to visit us. It was so good to see her because she was so cheerful, and helped us through a rough time.

Marinus phoned the hospitals in Edmonton, but none of them had room to take us, so Lori and I were air-ambulanced to the Foothills Hospital in Calgary.

All I remember of the next 10 days is extreme pain. They were giving me large doses of morphine, but all it did was muddle my mind up and didn't take the pain away at all. I could not even stand the weight of a sheet on my toes. I had excruciating pain from my pelvis to my toes.

Marinus did not feel comfortable with the doctor that consulted with him. The doctor seemed very arrogant and would not explain my situation to Marinus but insisted on talking to me about it. I was not coherent enough to understand what he was saying or make any decisions about my care. Marinus found out from Marilyn Steele, Barbie's mother-in-law, that her nephew, Stephen Miller, was an orthopaedic surgeon. He was on holidays but would be returning the following weekend. Marinus decided to wait and get a second opinion from him. On looking back, how very grateful I am for that decision my husband made for me.

I was operated on by Dr. Miller on August 29th. He built me a new L1 vertebrae with bone from the bone bank. He put in two bars and four screws to hold the bone in place. Two days after my operation, I tried to walk again. I remember being so very weak. I had to wear a brace to keep my back in place and this had to be put on while lying down. At first, the nurses did it up for me, but I knew they wouldn't let me leave the hospital if I couldn't do it for myself so I practiced and practiced. It was like trying to thread a sewing machine with my eyes closed. It sometimes took me over an hour to do it up, but I persevered.

My first steps were very difficult ones for me. My feet just didn't seem to go where I wanted them to go. The nurse that helped me was very brusque and unkind. She yelled at me and ridiculed me when I would step on my own toes. She kept kicking my feet apart. After our first session, I sat down on my bed and tried hard to hold back the tears. A very warm and caring nurse came in to me, put her arm around me and told me not to take any notice of the other nurse. This kind nurse said that she was very proud of me and happy with the progress I was making. I am grateful for both of these nurses and the lessons they taught me. I came to realize that the seemingly unkind nurse was only trying to help me, and because she made me a little angry, I think I tried harder than I perhaps would have if she had been more kind. I was able to learn how to walk well enough — even up and down stairs — so that I could go home two weeks after my operation.

My bladder and bowels both returned to normal function — much to Dr. Miller's amazement.

Many people visited me and sent cards to me during my time in the Foothills Hospital. My dear husband never left my side except to get a few hours of sleep each night.

When I was able to leave the hospital, Marinus took me home to Edmonton. I was nervous when I first got in the car, but we had a safe trip. We went directly to Si's room when we reached Edmonton, because I had to see for myself that he was all right. He was very happy to see me. We had both been worrying about the other, and it was good to see for ourselves that all was well.

At our Stake Conference in September, Elder Lorne C. Dunne was our visiting General Authority. On Saturday, he and President Higginbothom came to our home to visit me. When President Higginbothom phoned to see if they could come, I thought they were coming to see Marinus about a calling. I just couldn't believe they were coming to see me! I had a wonderful visit with them. I was able to go to conference and President Hudson asked me to say the opening prayer. It was hard for me to go up to the front, but I am grateful for the opportunity they gave me to do that, and I felt the spirit close to me as I gave the prayer. After the session, Brother Dunne asked Si if he could use another blessing. He gave Si the most beautiful blessing of comfort and healing, and he blessed me through Si, that my back would be completely healed.

31
THE MOVE

Early in the spring of 1991, Marinus received word that a new position in LDS Social Services was being opened in Regina. He wasn't going to tell me about it because he thought we couldn't possibly live anywhere else with Si, but one day he just mentioned it in passing. Imagine my great surprise when I found myself saying, "I think that is something we should look into." My husband was quite shocked, too, because I always said I would never leave Edmonton, mainly because of Si and the care he received there, but also because Edmonton is my home. But as soon as I said that to Marinus, I felt that this was what Heavenly Father wanted Marinus to do and where we should be serving.

A few little miracles happened after that. Marinus was able to receive the salary he needed and was accepted by those over him in LDS Social Services on his own reputation without even having an interview, (thanks to the recommendation of Brother Dallas Thompson, who was the Director of LDS Social Services for Alberta, and for whom Marinus had been working since January).

Marinus and I went to Regina at the end of May and found ourselves a lovely home at 11 Dalhousie Way in University Park.

We sold our home in Edmonton and moved to Regina on July 13th. Lori, Brian, and Benjie came to help us unpack and get settled in our new home. Our plan was that Marinus would stay in Regina to work, and I would return to Edmonton to be with Si until there were people trained in Regina to help me care for him at home.

32

A CRISIS

On July 22nd, Benjie, Dougie, (our grandson), and I left Regina for Raymond, to take Dougie home on our way to Edmonton. Marinus stayed in Regina to work.

When we got to Lori's house in Raymond, there was a message for me to call the Aberhart. I phoned the hospital and talked to Si's friend, Ken Pollock, who was visiting Si. He said that Si was not responding very well. I asked him to have Si's Dad call me as soon as he got there. Frank called and also said that Si was grinding his teeth and grimacing but not responding when he was spoken to. Frank called Dr. Mann, the doctor on duty at the time, and Dr. Mann said that they had checked Si's Dilantin level and it was fine and that the sore around his trach was healing well. Si's Dilantin level was not a concern, at that time, and he did not have a sore around his trach, so Frank realized that Dr. Mann knew very little about Si's condition. He just thanked him and hung up.

Ben and I decided that we had better leave for Edmonton immediately. We drove all night and arrived in Edmonton at 5:00 a.m. I phoned the Aberhart and they said Si was sleeping, so I went to bed for a little while and then got up and went to the hospital.

When I walked into Si's room, he was grinding his teeth and mouthing, "Help, help!" I walked over to him and he did not even recognize me. His color was terrible and his lungs were so full of infection that it was bubbling out of the top of his trach. I immediately suctioned him, and I have never seen so much gross green junk come out of his lungs as came then. It took five suctions before I got it all out. His suction bottle was full to the top with this green mucus.

I went out to find Joyce, the charge nurse, but she was on her break. I asked the clerk to have her come to Si's room as soon as she returned. Si was not able to use his alarm or even click and he had been left alone in his room. I waited for an hour and still no Joyce. The only person that came into his room was a nurse to give him his tube feeding.

Si's hands were very swollen, and he had a cold sweat all over his face and arms. He was very clammy and cold. I was extremely concerned about him so I went out again to the desk to see if the charge nurse was back. The clerk said that she had given Joyce my message and she then went to find her for me.

Joyce finally came into Si's room and I said, "We have a very sick young man here, Joyce." She replied in a very snarly tone, "Well, we have done all the tests we can. What else do you want us to do?" I replied, "Joyce, you are the nurse so why are you asking me what I want you to do?!" I asked her, "If Si was your son, would you want him to just lie there and not have anything done for him?" I showed her the jar that the secretions from his lungs were suctioned into and she said, "Well, he's not growing anything new." I told her that there probably wasn't anything else for him to grow and that what he had was terrible. I also pointed out to her that his urine output the night before had been very low and concentrated and he was covered in a cold sweat. I then asked if I could speak to Dr. Brown, who was Si's regular doctor, and she said that he was not on service until September. I then asked to speak to Dr. York, and she said that he was not on service until August. I told her again that I really needed to speak with them, and she said, "I'm sorry, I cannot help you but I will let you speak to Dr. Mann." I told her that Dr. Mann did not know anything about Si, and I did not feel comfortable discussing this with him but she still refused to let me speak to Dr. Brown or Dr. York. I then consented to speak to Dr. Mann.

Joyce left the room to get Dr. Mann. She returned a few minutes later to tell me that Dr. Mann was on the phone at the front desk and that he wanted to speak with me. I told him about Si's condition, and he said that he would come right away. Joyce then told me that Dr. Mann had seen Si earlier and that he had responded perfectly normally to him. I told her that I had a hard time believing that because

Si had not responded to his Dad the night before, and he certainly was not responding now and I just didn't see how he could have become normal in-between those times. She still insisted that he had.

Dr. Mann poked his head in the door and said that he had an emergency upstairs and would be down shortly. When he returned, Joyce came in the room with him. Dr. Mann walked over to Si's bed, looked at him grinding his teeth and grimacing, and he said, "Oh, he is responding the same way he did this morning." At this point, I had a hard time not telling Joyce exactly what I thought of her.

Dr. Mann also said that Si's tests were back. His sodium level was very low and he needed an IV started immediately. I asked if he could be sent to the main hospital ICU and he agreed that that was a good idea. I was so relieved.

Both he and Joyce then left Si's room and I never saw either of them again except when Joyce poked her head in the room to tell me that the ambulance would be there at 3:00 p.m. She never took Si's blood pressure or temperature and she never told anyone else to do it either.

Art, the orderly, came in and asked if I would like Si to have a bath before he went and I said yes. They took him for his bath. After his bath, they settled him back into his bed. Art felt that someone should check his blood pressure. It was 80 over 10. He ran out to get someone else to take it, and they could not get a higher reading either. As I said before, from the time I got there at 8:00 a.m. until just before Si left for the main hospital at 3:00 p.m., no nurse came in to check his condition. I felt that this was gross negligence on Joyce's part.

We took Si by ambulance to the main hospital, and he was put in a room on Station 5D3. The nurses there were very upset at his condition and wondered why no vital signs were taken and recorded and why he had not been brought sooner. His blood pressure was 78/38 and his temperature was 31 degrees C. After much poking, they got an IV started in his foot and they took some blood for further tests. They found that his blood protein and haemoglobin were both very low and his electrolytes had bottomed out. They gave him two units of blood and two more later that day and they started antibiotics for his massive urinary tract infection and for the pneumonia in his lungs. He was in septic shock.

He continued grinding his teeth all that day and all that night. He slept very little. On Wednesday, July 30th, at about 11:00 p.m., a resident doctor came in and said they were very concerned because his blood pressure was still dropping and they needed to get more IV lines going into him so they could give him Dopamine very quickly. She asked permission to have him moved to the ICU. We moved Si to the ICU at 12:30 a.m. They wouldn't let me in to see him for a couple of hours until they got the IV's going. He seemed to recognize me when I finally was able to go in, and he didn't seem as upset. I left him and went home around 3:30 a.m.

His condition stayed almost the same until the following Monday when he seemed to get much better. His body was very swollen, but his mind was clearer. They moved him into a private room in the ICU so that he could get some sleep.

Dave McTavish and Brigham Card came to see him on Saturday afternoon and gave him a blessing. Some time early Tuesday morning, Si went into a deep sleep and we couldn't wake him up. Finally, about 5:30 p.m., I was getting concerned that he might be in a coma so I raised his arm up to make him spasm. He opened his eyes and kept saying, "I'm fine, I'm fine" over and over again. He certainly was not quite right. He then went back to sleep and except for opening his eyes occasionally, he did not respond. He was much more swollen, and the doctors were concerned that he might have another massive infection somewhere in his body, because his lungs were much clearer than before.

They took some x-rays and planned to do a CT scan of his kidneys the following day. When I arrived at the hospital on Wednesday morning they had removed Si's G-tube because it wasn't working. They had put a tube down his nose to give him some dye, so they could do the CT scan. They stopped his Dilantin and his Baclofen. His Dilantin level was way too high, and they felt his baclofen level must also be too high because he wasn't having any spasms. I told them that I didn't think that they should stop the baclofen abruptly, because he might have a seizure. They assured me that his dylantin level was so high that he would not have one. I sure hoped they were right. I wished they would have Dr. Lakey, Si's urologist, look at him. I felt so sure that something was wrong in his kidney again and that Dr. Lakey would find it. I prayed that whatever was wrong would show up on the CT scan. He'd had six units of blood and they gave him two more that day. His blood pressure dropped again, so they gave him epinephrine to bring it up.

Marinus called to tell me that he had talked with Heavenly Father in his prayers, and he was told that Si would be all right. The doctors would be able to identify and treat the problem, and Si would be able to move to Regina. He said that the work that we would do in Regina was a very important work, and all three of us would be blessed so that we could do it. I told this to Si and I hoped that he was able to hear me and that it brought comfort to him, as it did to me.

Sunday, August 4, 1991 was a good day! When I went up to Si that morning, his eyes were open, and he seemed to be looking at me. I asked him how he felt, and he very slightly started to move his lips. I asked him again, and he mouthed, "I am fine". I was so happy I started to cry. Oh, how I loved this beautiful, courageous son of mine. I told him I loved him and he said, "I love you, too". He was getting better! How very thankful I was for the blessings that were mine — for the Priesthood's power and for doctors and nurses and medical technology that helped my son to live.

The CT scan they did on Si didn't really show anything. They talked with Dr. Lakey — Si's urologist — and they decided not to remove the stint in his kidney because they were afraid of spreading the infection. They had four antibiotics running into Si by I.V, all at once, and they wanted to see if this would clear up the problem. They gave him two more units of blood that day, and they also gave him a diuretic to get rid of the fluid. They took him off the epinephrine, and his blood pressure stayed up. He certainly seemed to be on the mend. I was so grateful to my Heavenly Father for hearing and answering our prayers.

On Monday, August 11th at 11p.m., they decided to move Si back to Unit 5D3. I was sitting by him waiting for them to get everything ready, when I suddenly noticed that his chest was not moving. I called the nurse, and she listened to his chest and confirmed that very little air was going in. I checked his volumes and he was getting about 200 cc's of air. He usually breathes on 800 – 850 ccs. I thought perhaps his left lung had collapsed, so I didn't dare bag him. They sent for the pulmonary resident doctor, and he was baffled. I suggested they x-ray his lungs, and they said they would move him first and x-ray him on unit 5D3. I told him I didn't think Si could go that long on 200 ccs of air. I felt so afraid and frustrated because no one seemed to be doing anything. Si's chin was moving like he was really air hungry, but I think he passed out because he didn't respond to me when I talked to him. Finally they agreed to do the x-ray there and sent me out of the ICU.

As I sat outside of the ICU, I prayed with all of my heart and pleaded with my Heavenly Father that if it were His will, that Si's life would be spared. I felt so alone and afraid, and then my thoughts turned to all of the beautiful blessings that Si had received and all the promises that had been made, and a sweet peace and calmness filled my heart. I knew that he was in our Heavenly Father's care and I didn't have to worry. How very grateful I am for that peace and assurance that came to me.

About an hour later, the doctor came out and said that they had found the problem. The problem was not with Si's lungs but with the filter on his machine. The filter had filled with water and mucus, so no air was able to go through it. They changed the filter and his pressures and volumes returned to normal. They also x-rayed his chest, and the doctor took me to a room in the back of the ICU and showed them to me. Si's lungs had greatly improved from the week before.

We then transferred him back to 5D3. I stayed with him until 2:30 a.m. Ben came and drove me to my car, which was parked at the Aberhart Hospital, so I wouldn't have to walk alone in the dark. I really appreciated his kindness to me.

I spent all day Tuesday with Si until 4:00 p.m., when I went to pick Marinus up at the airport. We then went directly to Si, and Marinus gave him a beautiful blessing of healing and comfort. I was grateful for the Priesthood that my husband held and honoured.

We went home briefly to eat dinner and when I returned, Si's father was there with him. As soon as I walked in the room, I noticed that Si's chest was not moving properly and his pressure was way up. It was supposed to be on 40 and it was on 48. The nurse called the respiratory technician. I took Si's volumes and he was only getting 400 cc's of air. This time I knew it was the filter. They changed it and everything returned to normal.

Si was still very swollen at this time. His cut downs on his arms had even broken open and were oozing fluid. He looked like he weighed 300 lbs. They started him on another diuretic, and it worked very quickly. By Thursday, the swelling had reduced greatly. The diuretic they used was called Lazix. The next day, however, he broke out in a severe rash all over his body from his chin down to his pelvis. It was a wet rash and was weeping badly. The doctors thought he might be allergic to the last antibiotic they had given him, so they discontinued it.

During the next week, the rash on Si's body slowly cleared up but he looked like he was turning into a fish. He was covered with scaly, dry skin.

From Tuesday until Sunday Si did not shut his eyes at all. He was not agitated, but he was really hallucinating. I'm not sure why this happened but I think it was a reaction to all the drugs that he had been given.

On Sunday, his home teachers, Bob Postma and Brother Kortniak, came up to bring him the Sacrament and I asked them if they would give him a blessing. Brother Postma blessed him and asked Heavenly Father to help him sleep. Early Monday morning, Si's eyes finally closed and he slept for two hours. After that, he slept very well.

Dr. Lakey changed the stint in Si's kidney to a larger one. He said he was surprised at how clean the old stint was and how clear Si's kidney was. I was so thankful that his kidneys had not caused the problem.

His body was quite healthy again. Another miracle had occurred in Si's life, and I was sure it wouldn't be the last.

I was so very grateful for the power in fasting and prayer. I was also very grateful for the knowledge that our Heavenly Father had given the medical profession, so that my Si could be helped.

33
THE MEETING

On Friday, August 23, 1991 I met with the patient Ombudsman at the University Hospital. She was a very nice person and listened intently to my concerns about the care Si had been given in the Aberhart. She seemed very appalled at the condition I found him in when I returned from Regina. She said she would meet with the director of nursing, Mrs. Payne, as soon as she returned from her time of bereavement. Mrs. Payne's husband had died the previous week.

A few days later, she phoned to say that she had arranged for me to have a meeting with Dr. Brown, Dr. Mann (this was a different person than the Dr. Mann in the Aberhart), Joanne — the ICU charge nurse, Joyce — the Aberhart charge nurse, and Mrs. Rempell — the assistant director of nursing for the Aberhart. This meeting was held on August 29th.

Dr. Mann took charge of the meeting and outlined the precarious nature of Si's health. Dr. Brown then outlined all the things they were going to do, in the future, for Si at the Aberhart. I told him I was glad for that because I didn't want to have a repeat of what had happened in July. I knew that Dr. Mann wanted me to bring this up so that it could all be out in the open. He asked me if I could tell them what had happened.

I then went over it all again. Mrs. Rempel interrupted me when I told them what Joyce had done, or not done, and she said that that was not the way she had heard it. I told her that I didn't know what she had heard, but I was telling her exactly what had happened. Joyce interrupted and said, "I called the doctor for you as quickly as you asked me to." I told her I appreciated that, but it should have been done much sooner.

They let me have my say and then Dr. Mann asked Joyce if she wanted to say anything. She asked me if there was someone at the Aberhart that I felt I could talk to easily and confide in. I thought about this for a moment and then I said, "Yes, Joyce, there are many people at the Aberhart that I can talk to freely, but the person I need to talk to and should talk to and want to talk to, is you! You are the nurse in charge." The look on Joyce's face was priceless. I was sure that after all that had happened she thought I would never talk to her again. She then said that she would like that, too, but wondered if our relationship had deteriorated too much for this to be possible. Dr. Mann quickly spoke up and said, "Joyce, you are being given another chance and I think you had better take it!"

As everyone rose to leave, I told Joyce that I was sorry that this situation had happened. She hugged me and said she understood because she had just gone through a similar situation with her own mother and assured me that things would be better.

We decided to take Si to Regina for his holiday instead of to Victoria as we had planned. That way Si would be able to see our new home in Regina.

Finally, in September, Dr. Mann felt that Si was well enough to leave the hospital. His health had improved greatly, and he was really excited to finally be able to leave the hospital after being confined for so many months.

34
SI'S REGINA VISIT

The home that we had bought in Regina was a perfect place for Si. There was a large family room right off the kitchen that we made into Si's room. It had wide sliding doors looking out to our beautiful back yard and a large deck where Si loved to sit and enjoy the sunshine.

The day after our arrival, we were sitting out on the deck. Our next door neighbour was working in her yard. She waved and said hello. She was wearing shorts and a tee shirt. In a little while, she went into her house and came back out, a second later, all dressed to go shopping. Si and I just stared in disbelief. Si said, "How did she do that Mom?" I told him I had no idea. She started to laugh and then an identical person came out of the house wearing the shorts and tee shirt. We lived next door to identical twins, June and Joan Le Page. They came over and introduced themselves and said they always enjoyed playing that little trick on everybody they could. We had a good laugh together.

Si enjoyed really good health for the first few days of his holiday, and then one day he went into a very bad seizure. I called an ambulance, and we took him to the Regina General Hospital. We weren't sure what caused it, but he recovered quickly and was able to return home the next day. We had no further incidents and spent a relaxing week together in our new home.

When it was time to return to Edmonton, we decided to leave quite early on Monday morning, so we could get to Edmonton in the afternoon and not have to travel in the dark. It was an eight hour trip from Regina to Edmonton. I phoned the Aberhart, just before we were ready to leave to tell Joyce that we would be there around 4:00 p.m. She said that we couldn't do that because she needed to be there when we arrived, and her shift ended at 3:00 p.m. We were a little upset because everything was packed and we were ready to leave. We decided to wait and leave at midnight so we would get there when Joyce was on duty at 8:00 a.m. We didn't relish the thought of travelling all night, but we didn't have much choice.

We arrived in Edmonton a little after 8:00 a.m. Marinus drove the van to the back door of the Aberhart so we could unload all of Si's equipment. We took Si out of the van, and I rang the bell to have someone open the door for us. Joyce and the nursing supervisor came to the door and said that we couldn't bring Si back to the Aberhart until he had been formally discharged from the University Hospital. I couldn't believe it! The Aberhart had been Si's home for over 16 years, and she would not let me take him to his room! I was so tired, I almost burst into tears. But I didn't. I just turned Si's wheelchair around and pushed him over to the University Hospital. I took him up to unit 5D3 where he had been before we went to Regina. I explained to the charge nurse why we were there, and she just couldn't believe that Joyce had made us do this. She said all it required was a phone call. She got some papers ready for me, and I wheeled Si back to the Aberhart. Joyce let us in. I got Si settled into his bed. He was very tired, but happy and grateful that he had had such a good holiday and a safe trip back to Edmonton.

35
THE OPERATION

On November 21st, Ben drove me to the Foothills Hospital in Calgary to have the appliances removed from my back that were put there at the time of my first operation. Dr. Miller operated on me again.

I had a terrible experience coming out of the anaesthesia. My lungs would not start working again on their own, and they had to wake me up so that I could fight to breathe. It was such a terrifying experience! My whole body was paralyzed, and I wasn't getting near enough air, and I had no way to tell them that. I guess my eyes must have been filled with terror, because the nurse asked me if I was getting enough air. He began bagging me harder, and I started to gag and choke and my lungs finally filled with air and I began to breathe on my own. I hope I never have to go through an experience like that ever again! I think I was given this experience so that I could empathize with Si more fully.

I slept most of the day of my operation, but I awoke at night and spent the hours until morning looking out of my window, watching the moon, and thanking my Heavenly Father for preserving my life.

The next morning Doctor Miller came in to see me. He sat on the side of my bed and looked at me for a few minutes, and then he said, "You know you are a miracle, don't you?" I said, "Yes, I am able to walk and run and take care of Si again, so I guess I am a miracle." He said, "Yes, but do you know that you are a 'real' miracle?!" I wasn't sure what he meant, but then he told me the most incredible story. As he related the following incident to me, he had tears in his eyes and had difficulty controlling his emotions.

He said that when he opened me up at the beginning of my first operation after the accident, he found such a big mess inside my back, that he didn't have the slightest idea where to begin. He said there were little fragments of bone everywhere, and he couldn't figure out why my spinal cord had not been severed. He said he was very afraid that he would paralyze me if he touched anything. He knew he needed help, so he prayed fervently to Heavenly Father to help him know what to do. He said that immediately it was revealed to him exactly what he was supposed to do. The whole procedure became clear to him. He built me a new vertebra with bone from the bone bank and then put in bars and screws to hold it in place until it healed.

How very, very grateful I am for the power of prayer, and that my husband insisted that Dr. Miller be the one to operate on me. If it had been the other doctor doing the operation, I know that things would not have worked out the way they did.

I spent the next month in Regina recuperating.

36

SI'S MOVE TO REGINA

On November 29th, Si went to the U of A Hospital and received a porta-cath. One of the veins in Si's upper abdomen was isolated and a device was put around it so that blood could be drawn and medications administered there. I was so very grateful that this was invented because Si's veins were very hard to find as he had cut-downs on all his major veins which made them impossible to access. The porta-cath made it so much easier for me to give him meds and to draw his blood while I cared for him at home in Regina.

Finally the day arrived for Si to move to our home in Regina. On December 19th, Marinus and I went to Edmonton to pick him up. When we got to the Aberhart, we found Si receiving antibiotics intravenously. They were being administered through his new porta-cath. Marinus and I had a meeting with Joyce, Elaine Remple, the nursing supervisor, and Dr. Brown. I had told them several weeks before, that we planned to move Si to Regina in December, but Joyce acted very surprised when we mentioned this and complained about not having any notice and wasn't sure if she could get the supplies ready. When I asked her how many days she could give us supplies for, she finally admitted that she had 5 weeks supply of everything ready for us. It just seemed that it was very hard for her to do anything without complaining.

Dr. Brown did not think that it was a good idea to take Si to Regina until he had finished his antibiotic treatments and suggested that we come back and get him on January 10th. I told him that we simply could not do that, and that I would learn how to administer his meds using his porta-cath.

A training session for the porta-cath had been held at the University Hospital in November, but I was unable to attend it. Joyce had said she would train me after I came back from having my back operation. She now said that she didn't have any time to do it.

When Dr. Brown realized that we were serious about taking Si, he suggested that the I.V. be heplocked until we got to Regina and asked Joyce if she would teach me how to mix his meds and administer them through the porta-cath. She did take time to help me and I had a very concentrated course in how to do these things. I had never done I.V. meds before, so it was a little scary, but I was grateful that she taught me and that I was able to learn how to do it.

It took us all day Friday and Saturday, December 20th and 21st to get all of Si's things loaded into a U-haul that Marinus would pull behind his vehicle. Finally, on Sunday December 23rd, after attending Sacrament meeting, we left for Regina. Ben drove the van, so I could take care of Si's needs while we traveled. We had a safe trip and arrived home late Sunday night, tired but happy.

I mixed Si's meds, and started his I.V. via the porta-cath and all went well. He was on three different antibiotics so it seemed like I was constantly mixing and administering meds for the next 10 days, but they did their job, and his lungs cleared up.

Si was so happy to be finally settled in our home in Regina.

37
REGINA EXPERIENCES

Our caregivers started on January 2, 1992. Evelyn was the first one to come and then Shirley started. Evelyn worked for about a month or so, and then she broke her foot, so Betty-Lou started. The caregivers came from 9:00 a.m. to 5:00 p.m. five days a week from January until November. During that time, I slept on a couch beside Si's bed each night so I could hear him if he needed me, and so I could turn him every two hours. The caregivers were not allowed to take care of Si alone, so I was never able to leave the house unless Marinus was home. For the first few weeks after we moved to Regina, different sisters from our Ward would stay with me at night if Marinus was out of town, so I would not be alone with Si. After a while, I felt more secure being by myself. In November, I changed the routine so that the caregivers came from midnight until 8:00 a.m. so that I could get a little more sleep. Our good friends, Jim Mason and Keith Greff, would come and help me lift Si into bed at night when Marinus was away.

We also had a caregiver, Gerald, and a VON Association nurse, Kathy, that came on Fridays from 6:30 to 10:30 p.m. so Marinus and I could have our date night. All the caregivers and people from the Ward that helped us were wonderful people. They really cared about Si and did so much for him. I will always be grateful for their love and caring concern.

Si loved to look out the big sliding door in his room and watch the seasons change. He often sat on the deck in his wheelchair and enjoyed the beautiful nature all around him.

In the spring, a couple of little grey birds with white breasts built a nest in the bird house on our back fence. Pretty soon six little baby birds emerged, and Si had a wonderful time watching them learn to fly. Our very large crab apple tree bloomed and looked like a huge, beautiful bouquet.

In April, Barb graduated from BYU, and I went to Provo, Utah to attend her graduation. Lori came to help Marinus care for Si while I was gone. One day, Marinus put on a tape of hymns and he and Si were both singing along with them as he cared for Si. One of Si's favourite hymns, "How Great Thou Art" was playing and when Lori looked at Si, he was singing along with all his heart, although he couldn't make a sound. This really touched her heart.

Si loved music and especially enjoyed singing the hymns. Our ward chorister, Maisie Lees Dodman, often told Si how much she appreciated watching him sing the hymns as she conducted on Sundays, because his eyes were always on her, and he knew every hymn by heart. She said she wished the other members of the congregation would do the same. Even though Si couldn't make a sound, he sang with all his heart, and his spirit rejoiced in the words and music of the hymns.

Ben and Rachel were married in the Salt Lake Temple on June 5, 1992. We took Si to the wedding. We had a safe and enjoyable trip there and back. I was so happy that Si was able be in the Temple with his 'little brother", and be a part of this special time in Ben's life.

Si loved the Temple and was able to attend many of them after he received his own endowment. He attended the temple in Cardston, Seattle, Idaho Falls, Provo, and Salt Lake. He had the wonderful privilege of witnessing the temple marriages of his brother David, his sister Barb, and his brother Ben. How grateful I was for my dear husband, Marinus, because without his assistance, Si would never have had the wonderful opportunity of attending the temple.

Si truly believed that 'men are that they might have joy', and he never lost his sense of humour throughout his many trials. He had a quick mind and could come up with incredibly funny one-liners at the drop of a hat.

One hot summer day in July Si wanted to sit out on the deck, so I put a long sleeved shirt on him, a hat, and some sun glasses, and he spent a few hours basking in the sun. That night when I got him undressed for bed I discovered that his hands, which had not been protected from the sun's rays, were very sunburned. When I told him they were sunburned he said, "Oh no Mom, you caught me red handed!" Si and his one liners!

Si often used his wonderful sense of humour to relieve a tense moment. One day our caregiver Betty Lou was helping me do Si's bowel routine. Betty Lou was holding him over on his side, and I was doing the necessary procedure, but it wasn't working very well. After a while, Si clicked to get my attention. I went around the bed so I could read his lips and he said, "Don't worry, Mom. It will all come out in the end." We had a good laugh. A few minutes later he clicked again and this time he said, "This is a real bummer!" We had another good laugh and a potentially embarrassing situation was eased.

We had a beautiful park not far from our home, and I would take Si for walks through it whenever he wanted to go. There was one part of the path that had quite a steep incline, and in order for me to push him up it, I would be almost flat out behind his chair. I would always sing the words from one of the pioneer children's songs "For some must push and some must pull as we go marching up the hill", whenever I pushed him up that hill, and one day a lady was coming down the path toward us and couldn't see me behind Si's chair. She thought Si was singing and was somehow getting himself up the hill. She was quite startled when she passed us and saw me behind his chair, and I was more than a little embarrassed, but Si thought it was really funny.

38

SI — THE MISSIONARY

Si was called to be the editor of the Regina Second Ward Elder's Quorum Newsletter. He really enjoyed this calling and besides editing the letter, he also contributed articles to it that he wrote on his computer. Following is one of the articles he wrote for this newsletter.

When the Prophet Commands — "Do It"

Many of us, lacking formal missionary training, hesitate to share the Gospel even though we have firm testimonies of its truthfulness. Three things that may keep us from sharing the gospel are: 1. Fear 2. Lack of experience 3. Lack of knowledge. How can we overcome these obstacles?

In Moroni 10:16 it says, "Perfect love casteth out all fear." If we can think more of the other person's salvation than our own feelings of fear, our fear will leave us. It may also help us to remember these words of assurance to us from the Lord, "I will be on your right hand and on your left, and my spirit shall be in your hearts, and mine angels round about you, to bear you up." Doctrine and Covenants 84:88

Missionary work, like so many other things in our lives, becomes easier as we do it more often. It is amazing how easy it really is to bring gospel beliefs into our conversations with people. We must constantly be aware of these opportunities and take advantage of them.

The world is becoming acquainted with Church standards and expects Latter-day Saints to live what they believe and teach. We must never underestimate the power of example. When we have doubts or become discouraged in our efforts we should remember His promise, "I will be with you; and in whatsoever place ye proclaim my name, an effectual door will be opened unto you, that they may receive my word." D&C 112:19

We will feel more comfortable in approaching people if we know and understand basic Church beliefs and doctrines well enough to bear testimony of their truthfulness. We do not have to be experts on all subjects, but what we share should be accurate. We must remember, however, that it is not our responsibility to convert the world single — handedly. Our responsibility is to find those who are ready to receive the message and then let the full-time missionaries do the teaching.

President Ezra T. Benson has asked us to flood the world with the Book of Mormon. When we feel hesitant about sharing this book with our friends and neighbours and acquaintances, we should ask ourselves, "If not from me — then from whom?" and then think of where they could wind up if we don't share the truth with them.

I bear witness that this is the Lord's true church and we have a responsibility to share this truth with others, so let us remember the urging of one of our Prophets and just, "Do it!"

Si really practiced what he preached. He would rarely leave our home without a copy of the Book of Mormon on his chair beside him, (just in case he found someone who didn't have one!) Well, he always seemed to find someone, and was able to give many copies of this great book to others.

He enjoyed sharing the Gospel whenever he had the opportunity, and sometimes he even made these opportunities happen. He would write out articles on his computer about the Book of Mormon, and then he would ask his caregivers to read what he had written onto a tape for him, supposedly so that he could listen to it them later. After I noticed the third caregiver reading the same article into the tape recorder, I realized what he was really doing — his missionary work.

This is the article that he had them read.

THE BIBLE AND THE BOOK OF MORMON

There are several scriptures talking about the Book of Mormon in the Bible.

In Ezekiel 37:16-17 it says, "Moreover, thou son of man, take thee one stick and write upon it for Judah, and for the children of Israel his companions: then take another stick and write upon it for Joseph, the stick of Ephraim and for all the house of Israel his companions: And join them one to another into one stick: and they shall become one in thine hand".

The stick of Judah is the Bible and the stick of Joseph is the Book of Mormon.

In the book of Isaiah, chapter 29, there are several references to the Book of Mormon. Isaiah saw the coming forth of the Book of Mormon as the voice of one that has a familiar spirit. It has a familiar spirit because, like the Bible, it contains the words of the prophets of God.

Another scripture talking about the Book of Mormon is found in Psalms 85:11, where it says, "Truth shall spring forth out of the earth and righteousness shall look down from heaven." We believe this is referring to the Book of Mormon because we believe the book is scripture from God our Father. Also, the records from which the Book of Mormon was translated were buried in a stone box in the earth, and were brought forth by the power of God to the Prophet Joseph Smith.

Then in John 10:16 it says, "And other sheep I have which are not of this fold, them I must bring also, and there shall be one fold and one shepherd."

In 3Nephi 15:21 in the Book of Mormon, the Saviour tells the people that they are the other sheep that He was referring to.

When Si was in the Aberhart, he shared the Gospel with his night nurse, Joanne Devenham, as she turned him in the night. She took the discussions and she and her daughter were baptised.

Reg Tiernan, a blind man who worked in the CNIB concession in the Aberhart, would go into Si's room and visit with him each day when he finished his work. He also took the discussions and was baptised.

Si was asked to give a talk in Sacrament Meeting in our Ward in Regina, on March 7, 1992. Marinus wheeled him to the front of the chapel and I read his talk for him.

Brothers and Sisters, I am grateful for the opportunity I have to speak to you today.

Seventeen years have passed since that eventful day — March 1, 1975 - when my world changed so suddenly. Because of the seriousness of my injury, I'm sure that many people, particularly those in the medical field, are very surprised that I am still here.

This mission that my Heavenly Father has given to me has brought many new experiences and opportunities for growth into my life that I probably would not have been able to have in other circumstances.

The thing that helps me most in my acceptance of my very limited physical abilities is the knowledge I have of the purpose of life and where it all fits in the eternal scheme of things. I try to keep an eternal perspective and as I have been able to do this, I have felt peace. I know that this life is only a small part of eternity and if I endure it well, I will be blessed and receive the reward I am striving for.

Another thing that has helped me is the complete trust I have in my Heavenly Father's will for me. He knows the things I need to experience on earth that will help me reach the potential He knows I can reach.

I also know that He will never give me more to bear than I can bear, with His help. As I have received strength from my Heavenly Father through His Priesthood's power, I have realized, anew, that my mission here on earth was fore-ordained, just like your missions were for-ordained, and that our lives will be preserved until we have completed these missions, if we are faithful. I also realized that the council given to the Prophet Joseph in liberty jail is true. In the Doctrine and Covenants 122:7 it reads, "Know thou my son, that all these things shall give thee experience and shall be for thy good."

For quite awhile after my accident happened, I didn't realize that I could do anything because of my very limited physical abilities, so I spent a lot of time watching T.V., listening to music, and working a little on my High School Correspondence Courses whenever a volunteer was available to help me. Then one day a young man named Duane Simpson — who had volunteered to help me with my Chemistry course — walked into my room and, in no uncertain terms, asked me what I was doing with my life, and challenged me to do something with it.

I realized then that, although my body was paralyzed, I still had my mind, and that my Heavenly Father expected me to use my time wisely, and to make the most of whatever circumstances I found myself in.

I received my Patriarchal Blessing and in it I was told that I must seek to know my Heavenly Father's will for my life. As I have received countless blessings from my Dad B. and others, my Heavenly Father's mind and will has been revealed to me a little at a time.

I have gained a great desire to learn, and I am grateful for all the many wonderful, unselfish people who have volunteered their time, over the years, to help me.

I am also grateful for those who have shown faith in my abilities and have given me opportunities to serve.

I appreciate the calling I have now in my Priesthood Chorum, and I am very grateful to be a Home Teacher. These activities really help to make my life more meaningful.

I was cautioned also, in my Patriarchal Blessing, to keep my mind free from evil or negative thoughts, and I have found that listening to the scriptures, talks of General Authorities, good books and good music have helped me do this.

I have come to love the scriptures and realize the great importance of studying them each day. I am grateful for the time I have each day to do that. Through them I have gained a great love for my Saviour, and a testimony of His life and mission.

I think of His birth — the most important event in the history of the world and the beginning of the greatest and yet most humble life ever lived.

I think of him as a boy, in the temple, listening and teaching, and how all who heard him were astonished by his understanding. I think of His three year mortal ministry and all that he accomplished in that short space of time. I am grateful that His teachings are recorded so that we can read and study them at anytime. But what is most marvellous to me is His great atoning sacrifice for you and me and everyone who has ever lived on the earth. This Atonement gives to all, immortality as a free gift, and offers to all, the hope of Eternal Life, or in other words — life with God.

How could he pay for all our sins and why did it make Him bleed at every pore? I thought long and hard on that. I really wanted to understand, so I thought of the things I had done wrong in my life and of all the sorrow and mental pain they caused me, and of the many nights I wet my pillow with my tears because of them (until I had repented of them). So now, each Sunday as I take the Sacrament, I think of the pain and sorrow these few sins caused me, then I try to imagine what it would be like if that pain was doubled, then tripled and so on, until it is too hard for me to think about. By doing this, I get a tiny glimpse of what he went through as he suffered for all.

When I think of these things, it makes me want to love Him and serve Him and keep his commandments. In fact it is a privilege for me to do so. That is how I feel about Him. I ask you to think about all that He has done for you, as you take the Sacrament each week.

I have a strong testimony of the Gospel and the truthfulness of the Church. I know Heavenly Father hears all of out prayers and answers them. I know He loves each one of us, as does His Son, Jesus Christ.

I say these things in the name of Jesus Christ, amen.

39

ILL HEALTH RETURNS

On August 16, 1992 Kelsey Leigh Ann Eakett was born to Lori and Brian. On August 24th, we put Si in the Plains Hospital for respite care so I could go and help Lori with her new baby.

I worried when I entered the room at the Plains Hospital because there was a peculiar odor and I was sure that some of the patients in the room had pseudomonas. I asked the nurse to please use very sterile procedures when suctioning Si so that he would not catch it. Si did quite well at the Plains, but he did get a bladder infection and a pseudomonas infection. That was the chance we took whenever we put him in the hospital.

Si's health continued to deteriorate, and he spent ten days in the General Hospital in September. They gave him medications by IV to help take away the lung and bladder infections he had.

He went really strange while he was there and was not able to talk to us. He just lay there and clicked constantly and ground his teeth. I'm not sure what caused it. I think it may have been his way of shutting himself off so he could stand the way they suctioned him and the terrible shortness of breath it caused. I don't know how Si bore the terrible trials he had to go through. I know his Heavenly Father helped him, or he would never have been able to stand it.

When he left the General Hospital, I felt that the infection was not gone and I asked if he could be on an oral antibiotic for a while, but they said it wasn't necessary. The infection did come back a few days after he came home.

Finally Dr. Ready ordered some Cipro antibiotic to be given to Si orally and, at first, it seemed to help, but after a few days the infection got worse. They upped the dosage from 500 mg pills to 750 mg pills and it still didn't help. I kept taking sputum samples and sending them into the lab and, after a few weeks, I was told to stop the Cipro because the infection was growing right through it. Dr. Ready said that I should start him on Ticarcillin IV but we couldn't find any of that medication anywhere in Regina. I told him that I had some Peprocil on hand, so he said to go ahead and start it.

I phoned the VON Association to see if they could send Kathy Craig to assist me in starting the IV but they said that they had to have orders from the doctor, Si's complete drug history, etc., before they would come, so I told them I would do it myself. The spirit guided me, and I was able to reconstitute the meds and get the IV started. I was so very thankful that I received this help and that I had a husband who stood by me and gave me the moral support I needed. I am also very grateful that Si had a porta-cath, because without that, I would not have been able to do this at home. Si's infections became somewhat better.

In November of 1992, Si's brother David graduated from the University of Alberta in Edmonton with a BA Degree. We decided to take Si to Edmonton so that he could see his brother graduate.

David, Marinus, and Si.

After the graduation ceremony, we all went to Frank and Jen's for dinner. It started to snow while we were there, and there were storm warnings. We decided to stay the night in Edmonton and leave very early the next morning.

The worst part of the trip was from Edmonton to Saskatoon. The storm was really very bad. There were many times, especially when cars would pass us, that we were in total whiteout. It was such a frightening experience. Finally, Marinus realized that if he stayed behind one of the big semi-trucks, it was easier to know where the road was. The only bad thing about that was, when we passed other vehicles, the snow would blow up around them and their drivers wouldn't be able to see where they were going and would drift over the line and almost hit us. It was so scary! We prayed before we left Edmonton and continually throughout the trip. Our Heavenly Father heard our prayers and answered them. The trip took us over 14 hours, but we reached Regina in safety, arriving home a little before midnight.

Evelyn came to be with Si during the night, and I was very thankful for the chance to rest.

Whenever Si was unable to go to Church on Sunday because of illness, the young Priesthood holders of the Ward would bring the Sacrament to him. Si was so grateful for this service and wrote the following letter of appreciation to the Bishop.

Dear Bishop,

I want to publicly thank the young men who bring me the 'Sacrament', and the other people who have served me since I came to Regina. These people are going to have so much of an advantage when the Saviour comes again, for the Saviour of us all has said, "In as much as ye have done it unto one of the least of these, my brethren, ye have done it unto me."

I want to tell you why I feel so strongly about taking the Sacrament. It is because, without the Saviour's atoning sacrifice for us, we would all be damned. The atonement was such an important part of the plan. It was revealed to the prophet Joseph Smith, "I, God, have suffered this for all mankind, so that they might not suffer if they would repent…"

Thanks again for bringing the Sacrament to me.

Sincerely,
Your friend,
Si Peterson

Si continued on IVs at home until December 15th. He started getting a little swelling, so Dr. Gulamali told me to take him to the General Hospital for Dr. Lynn, an infectious diseases doctor, to look at him. They did a blood culture while we were in the emergency department, and Dr. Lynn said that his infections were gone, and we could stop the IV. His electrolytes were out of whack, however, so they put him on phosphates, iron, and calcium supplements.

The pseudomonas returned very quickly, and I kept sending in sputum samples every week, but they said he wasn't growing anything new. He was just colonized, and his own body had to fight the infection. It just kept getting worse and worse.

One day, just before Christmas, I noticed that the right side of Si's face was drooping, almost as if he had had a stroke. That side of his mouth didn't move very well, so it was hard to read his lips. Through all of this suffering, he never complained. He continued to try to work on his computer every day and spent many hours listening to the scriptures and other good books. Time was precious to him, and he always tried to fill it with worthwhile things.

40

THE VISIT

January 1993 – The infection in Si's lungs kept getting worse and worse. He had to be suctioned every 5 to 10 minutes day and night. He was short of breath a lot and just did not feel well at all. It was so hard to see the suffering he was going through. Finally, on January 13th, I called Len at the ARS Office and asked if he could do something to help Si breathe better. When he came, he said that Si had severe pseudomonas and probably other infections and should be in the hospital. He adjusted Si's ventilator to give him 1200 ccs of air at 10 to 11 breaths per minute. Si was usually on 900 ccs at 14 breaths per minute. The deeper breaths seemed to help him for a while.

Marinus had been gone for about 10 days visiting his mother in Victoria. It was hard having him gone for so long. I really missed him. Yvonne Larson stayed at our home overnight on the days that our caregivers didn't come. I really appreciated her doing this for me. Marinus arrived home on January 14th, and I was so very happy to see him.

My friend Rini West had been having severe headaches for quite a long time. She called me that day and asked if I could watch the children while she went to the doctor. When Rini and Norm got back to pick up the children, Bishop Taylor and Jim Mason came to give her a blessing. Marinus actually gave the blessing, assisted by the Bishop and Jim. They then came into Si's room and Bishop Taylor gave Si a most beautiful blessing. He then gave me a blessing.

The Spirit was so strong in our home that night. I am very grateful for the great power that is in the priesthood and for men that hold and honour it.

That evening, Dr. Gulamali called and said that she had arranged for Dr. Abdula to see Si in Emergency on Monday, January 17th. Len had called her to tell her how sick Si really was.

As I look back on it now, I wish with all my heart that I had over-ruled her diagnosis of Si's condition and taken Si to the hospital much sooner.

On Saturday night Si's condition was not very good, so Marinus gave him another blessing. He blessed him that he would be able to have a good night's rest and that his breathing would be easier. Marinus also gave me a blessing, so that I would have the strength to care for Si and would feel calm about the lesson I was to give the next day in Relief Society. He also said that before the night was over, I would receive a special sign that would help me to realize more fully that my Savior lives and loves me and that my Heavenly Father was watching over us.

When Marinus finished giving me my blessing, he said, "Now, who gives me a blessing?" and Si said, "I will."

Early in December, Si's face had stopped moving and only the right side had recovered, so it was really hard to read his lips. Marinus and I both felt that even if I couldn't read his lips, it was still very important for him to give the blessing. Marinus held Si's hands on his head, and Si gave Marinus a beautiful blessing of comfort. I know it was a beauti-ful blessing because the Spirit was so strong.

Marinus then went off to bed and Si continued needing suctioning about every five minutes. Finally, at 4:00 a.m., I sat down on the couch beside Si's bed and cried out to my Heavenly Father, "Why are you not answering our prayers? Why do you not acknowledge the many bless-ing that have been given?" It seemed to me that the heavens had closed and that nothing was getting through. Suddenly, I felt this peaceful feeling come over me, and I laid my head down and fell instantly asleep. I awoke at 6:00 a.m. Si was still sleeping peacefully. I suctioned him as quietly as I could and he continued to sleep until 8:30 a.m. I had received the sign that had been promised in my blessing. My heart was full of gratitude to my Savior and to my Heavenly Father. I knew that they were watching over us, and had heard my pleas and answered me.

My lesson that day in Relief Society was on "Living in the Dispensation of the Fullness of Times". To begin my lesson, I told the sisters about my experience the night before, and told them that sometimes things have to get really dark before our Heavenly Father sends his light and understanding. It was during the darkest times of our Prophet Joseph's life that he received the most light. It was during a time of terrible persecution that he received all the keys and powers to usher in the last dispensation. The Spirit was strong throughout the lesson and I was very grateful for that.

Marinus stayed home with Si while I went to my meetings. I appreciated the unselfish service that he always gave, and especially during this very difficult time.

We had another incredibly wonderful experience happen that evening.

Si was having a very difficult time breathing again and no matter what I did, I could not help him to be comfortable. I phoned Len at ARS and asked him what I should do. He said that he didn't have any suggestions and advised me to take him to the hospital immediately. Si's lips were very blue and he was going through a terrible struggle. I went into the dining room where Marinus was writing in his journal, and told him what Len had said. Marinus reminded me that Dr. Abdula was not on call and that if I took Si to emergency, he would just lay there all night and nothing would be done for him. Shirley was coming in to care for Si during the night, so Marinus felt that we should keep Si at home, so that I could get a good night's sleep to be able to cope with whatever the next day would bring. I expressed my concern about Si not being able to breathe very well, and Marinus told me that I needed to turn it over to the Lord. When he said this to me, I felt rather angry toward him because I felt that he thought I didn't have any faith. I knew that Si was in Heavenly Father's care, but I couldn't just walk away from him and say, "I'm sorry you aren't breathing very well Si, but you are in the Lord's hands." I felt that Heavenly Father expected me to do as much for Si as I could, even though I knew that He was over all. I said all this to Marinus in a rather cross voice and then Si clicked, so I went back to him.

I could not believe the change that had come over Si! It was a miracle! He was totally calm and his face looked so beautiful and peaceful and his lips were no longer blue. He said to me, "Don't worry, Mom. I am all right. The Saviour is here and He is helping me. He asked me to tell you to go to Marinus and apologize to him for speaking to him in a cross way." I could hardly believe what I was witnessing. I immediately went to Marinus and told him what had happened and what Si had said.

What a very humbling experience that was for me. I learned three very important lessons from it. I learned that when you have done everything you can, that is in your power to do, that the Saviour will make up the rest. I learned that those who honour His Son, the Father honours. I also learned that our Saviour and our Heavenly Father care about the way we speak to each other. I shall always be grateful for the wonderful lessons that I was taught that night. Si was not short of breath and slept well the whole night. A most wonderful miracle had occurred!

41

THE END

The next morning, Si was taken to the General Hospital by ambulance. Evelyn came early to help me get Si ready. We washed him, shaved him, took care of his sores, and did his bowel routine. We got to the Emergency at the General Hospital at about 10:00 a.m.

We were supposed to meet Dr. Abdulla there, but we never did see him. They took blood from Si and did x-rays. At 4:30 p.m. we finally took Si up to the ICU. On the way up, the respiratory technician was bagging Si and doing a very poor job of it. He wasn't giving Si nearly as much air as he needed. Si was really suffering. I told the technician that Si needed much bigger breaths so he would bag one hard one and then go back to shallower ones. By the time we got to the ICU, Si was having a very hard time. The charge nurse came in and asked me to wait in the lounge. I told her that I would very much appreciate it if she would let me stay with Si. She was not happy with this, but she did not make me leave. We got Si into bed and then his nurse told me that they had rules here and that family members wait in the lounge while certain procedures were being done. I told her that this was probably fine for most families, but that I was Si's chief caregiver and that there were not too many procedures that I had not done already for him, myself.

She left the room and came back a few minutes later to tell me that I was not to bag Si or suction him or do any other care for him. I said, "That's fine. I am not here to do that anyway. I am here to give Si emotional support".

I think they soon realized that that was not a smart decision on their part because Si needed suctioning every few minutes. Every time the mucus gurgled up, I went to the door of Si's room and told them that he needed suctioning. After a few hours of this, one of the nurses came in and said that it was alright with Dr. Gibbings if I suctioned, but they were trying to convince the charge nurse that this was alright for me to do. I told her that they didn't have to convince her because they should be suctioning him.

The next day, Si had a very young nurse caring for him. She approached me as I was coming in from the lounge and told me that it was alright for me to suction, if I let her observe me doing it so that she could see that I knew how to do it properly. I didn't know whether to laugh or cry, but all I said was that it was their responsibility as his primary care-giver. It soon became apparent to me that there was a lack of understanding about how vital suctioning was for Si. Unfortunately for Si, I couldn't be there 24 hours a day to provide this care, as it was not being done properly or as often as he needed.

After doing many blood tests, etc., they determined that Si had pneumonia in both lungs and was growing five different organisms. He was an extremely ill person.

I didn't see Dr. Abdulla on Monday or Tuesday and I really needed to talk to him to find out what was going on. I phoned his office Wednesday morning and his nurse told me to phone back Wednesday afternoon. I did that, and she told me that he would see me in the ICU between 3:00 and 5:00 p.m. that day. He finally arrived at 5:30 p.m. He told me that Si was gravely ill and he asked me how hard I wanted them to try to save him if he should go into cardiac arrest. I told him that I wanted them to try as hard as if Si was his son and was a perfectly normal person. He thanked me, and when I went on to tell him about the special, intelligent person that Si was, he stopped me and said that he knew that, and that I didn't have to say any more about it. He didn't sound too optimistic that Si was going to make it through this illness. I assured him that I felt Si would come through it all, but he still seemed very sceptical.

I taught two of the doctors how to access Si's porta-cath. They put him on three different antibiotics and gave him eight units of blood over the next week.

His electrolytes and his haemoglobin became quite normal again. The second day that he was in the hospital, he began to swell up. They gave him albumin and a blood thinner to take the fluid away. After about a week, the swelling started to go down, and I felt that Si might be able to go home the next week.

We had several scary episodes during the next few weeks. Early Thursday morning, January 20th, Dr. Abdulla called us in the middle of the night and told us that Si's blood pressure had bottomed out and they needed to start an IV line into the main vein into his heart. There was an anaesthesiologist there ready to insert the line and he explained the necessities and dangers of the procedure to me. I gave them permission to go ahead with it. Marinus and I got dressed quickly and arrived at the hospital around 2:30 a.m. We went right in to see Si and he didn't seem any worse to me than he had when I left him at 10:30 the night before. They explained that this procedure was also a precautionary measure, just in case he needed dopamine to be given rapidly. The line could also be used to measure his internal blood pressure.

We waited in the lounge for about an hour and then the nurse came and told us that they couldn't get the line in. Si was so swollen that they couldn't find the vein. Both Marinus and I felt that if they were able to do it, that would be fine, but if they couldn't do it, Si would also be all right. We both felt a sense of peace while we were waiting.

Dr. Gibbings was able to get the line in later, when she arrived. She put it in his leg up to his heart. His blood pressure was very low, so they were able to give him dopamine to bring it up. He hadn't produced any urine all day, but by the time we left the hospital at 6:00 a.m., he had done about 400 ccs.

About a week later, after the redness of the toxic shock lessened and his swelling started to go down, he suddenly developed a severe rash all over his body. When he was in toxic shock, his upper body looked like it had been scalded, but the rash that developed, from a sensitivity to the antibiotic Cipro, looked like a bad case of measles. His kidneys stopped working again, and they kept giving him Albumin and Bolus NaCl IV to try to trigger his kidneys to work. Unfortunately, all that happened was that he swelled even bigger. They discovered also that he was growing two new organisms, so they started more new antibiotics.

On Sunday, February 7th, Marinus and I planned to go to our Sacrament Meeting at 9:00 a.m., and then Marinus would go to Si while I taught my lesson in Relief Society, but when Marinus was backing the van out of the garage, he got stuck in a snow pile. A neighbour came and helped him get out, but by that time it was too late to make Sacrament Meeting, so we went directly to Si.

When we walked into Si's room, I could not believe the way he looked. His face was so swollen that he looked like a Neanderthal man. His eyes were swollen shut and his lips were huge. I had to turn away to regain my composure. I just wanted to hold him in my arms and cry. He was so patient through all of these trials. He just lay there and never complained.

I left him only long enough to give my lesson in Relief Society. Alex Clark and Glen Geisinger came up to give Si the sacrament. He was unable to take it, so they administered it to me. I am so grateful for these faithful young men who came up each week to give Si this sacred ordinance. Marinus and I stayed with Si until about 11:00 p.m. It was so hard to leave him. We fasted for Si that day, and Marinus gave Si a wonderful blessing.

On Monday, February 8th, Dr. Gibbings phoned from the ICU quite early in the morning and told me that Si did not have a good night. Dr. Gibbings had come about 3:00 a.m. to put another line in from Si's main vein in his neck to his heart, because his blood pressure had bottomed out again and his kidneys were not functioning. They also put a tube down his nose into his stomach to draw off the bile that was pouring out of his mouth and nose.

Marinus and I went up very early and found Si even more swollen than the day before. His lips were huge, and his skin was so taut that it looked transparent. His eyes were swollen tightly shut. His whole body, including his face, felt like a piece of wood. It would not dent at all. It was hard for me to imagine what his face must have felt like to him. He was the most courageous person I had ever known. Imagine lying there completely paralyzed, unable to move anything at all, not even your face or even open your eyes. What an incredibly scary experience that would be. My Si had been experiencing this for days and just accepted it calmly and with courage and faith.

Dr. Gibbings told us that things didn't look good for Si. She felt that the best treatment would be to do kidney dialysis. She said that they would have to wait until Tuesday to start it, because all of the dialysis nurses were busy. However, Linda, an ICU nurse from England, who had worked in dialysis for four years, volunteered to run the machine for Si that day.

They started the dialysis around 1:30 p.m. and should have been finished by 5:30, but the first machine broke down after only half an hour and the second machine wouldn't work well either. I began to pray really hard that they would not have to start another machine, because each time they did, Si would lose a lot of blood. The nurse was just starting to run the blood from the tubes back into Si so she could start the third machine when, all of a sudden, the machine began to work and never gave a minute's problem after that. My prayer had been answered.

With this dialysis, Si lost approximately 11 pounds. It was quite an experience to watch his lips go down and his face become smaller. It was truly a metamorphosis. I was so happy.

On Tuesday, February 9th, I got up at 4:00 a.m. to call the hospital to see how Si was doing, and they said that he was sleeping peacefully. I went back to bed and at 7:00 a.m. the phone rang and the nurse from ICU said that Si had just bled profusely from his lungs. His blood pressure had dropped drastically, and his heart rate was very low. Marinus and I dressed quickly and prepared to go to the hospital. I had very severe Cystitis, and my bladder was really burning, so Marinus gave me a blessing. He blessed me that my bladder would stop burning, and I would have the strength to be with Si and give him the support that he so very much needed. His prayer was heard and answered.

When we got in to see Si, he was once again quite stable. They were giving him platelets and later that day they gave him two units of blood.

On Wednesday, February 10th, they decided to do dialysis on Si again. He had a small bleed at about 9:00 a.m. I asked the nurse if Si's bleeding could have anything to do with the Heparin they gave him during the dialysis treatment to thin his blood. She said that it very definitely could be affected by that, so, in the middle of the dialysis treatment, she took a blood sample. It took 240 seconds for it to even start clotting. The normal clotting time is 30 to 60 seconds. She became quite alarmed and turned off the Heparin drip. After the treatment was over, the time was still quite high at 90 seconds.

My sister, Eltie, her husband Duke, and her son Ronnie-Duke, arrived at our house around 7:00 p.m. Eltie phoned the ICU to tell me that they were there. I left Si to go home around 10:30 p.m.

Si lost another 10 pounds of fluid the next day. He looked so much better. Almost like himself again. His kidneys still weren't functioning very well. He was only outputting about 300 ccs of urine in 24 hours. As the swelling went down, Si was able to see again, but I could tell that he wasn't quite right. He had a hard time focusing his eyes and he began to grind his teeth. This really worried me, so the nurse called a resident doctor to talk to me to explain Si's symptoms. He said that when a person loses that much fluid that rapidly, it usually makes them confused, but the confusion would go away after a few days. Si did not sleep a wink that night.

On Thursday, February 11th, Eltie and I spent the whole day with Si. He was still quite confused. He kept saying, "_____ Mom" and Eltie thought he was saying, "I love you, Mom." Oh how I hoped that that was what he was saying. I stood by him most of the day and stroked his hair to help him feel better. He still didn't sleep all that day.

Eltie and I went home at 6:00 p.m. to get supper. As we walked in the door, the phone rang. It was the hospital. Si had had another really bad bleed from his lungs, and his heart had stopped. We rushed back to the hospital. They wouldn't let us in immediately because they were cleaning him up. When we finally got in, he seemed quite normal except his blood pressure was a little low and his heart rate was up. I phoned Si's dad in Edmonton and explained the gravity of Si's current condition to him. He said that he, along with his wife Jen and daughter Trish, would come the next day.

Marinus was in Winnipeg. How I wished he was home so that he could give Si a blessing to help him sleep.

Frank, Jen, and Trish arrived on Friday, February 12th, in the afternoon. They came straight up to Si. Si was still a little confused, but he seemed to know who they were.

When I left Si at 11:00 p.m., he seemed quite stable, although he was still not passing any urine and was becoming very swollen again.

Marinus came home on Saturday, February 13th. He gave Si a blessing so he could sleep and he finally slept well. I was so grateful for the priesthood's power and for the many times it had helped Si through difficult situations and had brought comfort, peace and wellness to him.

They were going to do dialysis on Si again that morning, but I just didn't feel right about it because of his blood clotting factor, so I phone Dr. Gibbings at her home. She agreed with me and thanked me for calling her. I told her how grateful I was to have a doctor for Si who really cared. She said that they would start dialysis again on Monday.

Frank stayed with Si in the morning on Sunday, February 14th, so that Marinus and I could go to Church. When we got to Si after lunch, Frank said that Si had slept all night and had been asleep most of the day. I was so grateful that he was finally able to relax and sleep.

I invited Frank, Jen, and Trish to come to our house for supper that night. We had a good dinner together and were almost ready for our dessert when the phone rang. I answered it and the clerk at the ICU said, "One moment please, the charge nurse would like to speak to you."

I started to shake so badly that I could hardly hold the phone. It took several minutes before she came on the phone to tell me that Si had had another major bleed and that we had better come to the hospital. When I went into the dining room to tell Frank and Jen and Marinus, I got such a terrible pain in my back and chest that I could hardly breathe. I thought I was having a heart attack.

We rushed to the hospital, but they wouldn't let us in right away because they were cleaning Si up. When they finally let us in, we found Si to be remarkably well. His heart rate was 70 and his blood pressure was normal. He'd had a very bad haemorrhaging in his lungs, and his heart had stopped again. His eyes were swollen shut, but he was able to move his lips a little bit. I asked him if he was alright, and he said, "I feel really fine, Mom."

I couldn't believe that I was able to read his lips because I hadn't been able to read them at all for quite a while. I told Si that he was the bravest, most valiant, and faithful person that I had ever known and he said, "I have had a lot of help, Mom."

The nurse asked us to wait in the waiting room while a doctor tried to get another IV going so they could give Si some more blood.

We waited in the waiting room for about an hour. Finally they came to tell us that they couldn't get it going. I knew that Dr. Gibbings would be working in the morning, and she would be able to get it going because she was a genius at starting IV's.

We went back into Si's room and had a wonderful visit with him for several hours. He asked me to give Brent, the respiratory person, a copy of the Book of Mormon. When Brent left the room, I told Frank and Marinus what Si had said. Frank laughed and said, ``You won't stop until everyone has a copy of the Book of Mormon will you, Si'?" Si smiled. We had a really good visit talking about some of the clever one-liners that Si is so famous for. It was wonderful to be able to visit with him again and to be able to know what he was saying.

At about midnight, I selected a tape for Si and put his headphones on him. We said prayer together and then Frank and Marinus said goodbye to him and went out into the waiting room. I found a hymn tape for him that he could listen to when the other tape was finished. I then went to find Mike, his male nurse, to tell him to put it on when the other tape was done. I said goodnight to Si and told him that I really loved him. He said, "I love you, too, Mom``.

42

THE BEGINNING

(An entry from my Journal)

Monday, February 15, 1993 – *My Si Guy has gone.* Si passed away at 5:15 this morning. It is so hard for me to write these words because I never thought my Si would die. I truly believed, with all my heart, that he would be healed before the Saviour came and that all the blessings that had been promised so many times would be given here on the earth. I know there is an answer to it all and someday it will be made clear to me. I felt so peaceful when we left Si last night because he seemed so much better and we had such a wonderful visit together. How like my Si to always want to make things better and easier for others.

At 5:00 this morning the phone rang and I answered it. The voice on the other end said, "This is the ICU calling. Si has taken a very bad turn. You had better come".

I woke Marinus and we dressed as quickly as we could. I was shaking so badly that I could hardly get my clothes on. We arrived at the hospital at about 5:30. All the way there, I was praying so hard that Si would be alright, and that if he had passed away, Marinus would be able to bring him back through the Priesthood's power. I was shaking and yet I had a calm, peaceful feeling inside, and I knew that all would be well.

I phoned into the ICU from the waiting room and the clerk said that Si's nurse would be right out. I knew then that he was gone because usually they just asked us to wait while they cleaned Si up before we came in. Si's nurse, Mike Watson, and the charge nurse came into the lounge. Mike came directly to me and said, "We are so sorry. We did everything we could, but he just wouldn't come back." Mike was so kind and I felt bad for him that he had to be the one to break this sad news to us. He said Si was being cleaned up and that we could go in to him, in a few minutes. I told him that I really wanted to see Si now and it didn't matter to us if he was clean or not. We went right in to my dear Si and closed the curtains around us.

His respirator was gone and all the lines and tubes he had connected to him, before, were all taken away. It seemed so very strange to see him lying there without anything connected to him. It was the first time that I had seen him without a respirator for almost 18 years. He was still very swollen, but his face looked peaceful, as if he was just sleeping. I covered his shoulders with the sheet, because he always liked his shoulders covered. Marinus then anointed him with the consecrated oil, and then sealed the anointing with a beautiful blessing of healing. He prayed that, if it be our Heavenly Father's will, Si would return to his body and wake up. It was a short plea to our Heavenly Father for the return to life of our beautiful, valiant son that we loved so very much. Marinus was told, in his mind, to keep his hands on Si's head. He kept them there for quite a long time, and then, as nothing happened, he was told to remove them. He said that as he stood there with his hands on Si's head, he felt a tremble go through Si's body. We think that it was at this point that Si decided — that he made the decision — to not come back. His mission on this earth was completed. What a valiant, honourable mission it had been. We are sure that he stood there beside us, seeing clearly both paths and chose the one that led to the Spirit World and all the glorious possibilities that were there for him. What joy filled my heart for him. What indescribable sorrow filled my heart for me and my loss. Oh how I missed him! He had been an extension of me for 18 years and I felt as if half of my being had been torn cruelly away, leaving a big gaping empty hole. I thought my heart would break with the pain.

My dear husband put his arms around me and we stood silently saying our goodbyes to our son. The nurse came in and asked me if I would like to speak to Si's father. They had called the hotel where he was staying. Frank and I cried together for this son of ours and I knew he felt the loss as deeply as I did. I told him that the important thing now was for us to live our lives in such a way that we would be able to be with him again someday. He said, "Yes, I know."

I went back to Si and kissed him and stroked his hair as I had done so many times throughout his life. Si's earthly mission was over. The words that President Tanner had said in the blessing he gave to Si, shortly after his accident happened, came into my mind. 'Your days were set before you came to the earth and they will not be numbered a day less'. Si is not dead. He is healed. He is walking. He is talking. He is sharing the Gospel freely and without restraint. Peace began to come.

(End of journal entry)

When we got home from the hospital, my sister Eltie was there waiting for us. I was so grateful she was there. Her presence gave me so much comfort. It was almost like having my Mom there with me. We cried together as I told her the things we had experienced. Frank and Jen and Trish came over, and we all hugged and cried together, too. How thankful I am that they were able to be there and that we could share this sad, but beautiful, experience together and give strength and comfort to each other.

They had to catch a plane back to Edmonton that afternoon, so we all went to the funeral home to pick out Si's casket and make arrangements to have his body taken to Edmonton for the funeral.

The casket that Frank liked best was made of copper and was the most expensive one there. I liked one that was made of oak and was $2000 cheaper. I kept thinking how happy Si would be if we got the cheaper one and used the money, saved, to help someone in the mission field. Material things were never very important to Si. I quickly realized, however, that it was very important to Frank to get the best for Si, so I agreed on the copper one. It was truly a beautiful coffin, and I am grateful that my Si was laid to rest in the best that we could get for him.

Marinus phoned all of our children and also called Derrel Hudson in Edmonton to arrange for the funeral.

Several people came to our home that afternoon to offer their con-
dolences. One of Si's special friends, Jim Mason, came. This was very
hard for him because he loved Si and visited him and helped me with
him so many times.

Many people phoned offering their sympathy and love. I have rarely
seen such an outpouring of love and concern as was shown to us.

Sister Geisinger and her son Ryan came to visit. When Ryan came
in, I looked at him and I realized that Si was standing now and he was
tall, like Ryan. I told this to Ryan and how I wished I could see my Si
and give him a big hug. Ryan said that he would like to give me a hug if
that would help me. I said it would, so he gave me a great big hug. He
told me that anytime I needed a hug, I just had to let him know and he
would give me one. And he kept his promise. Whenever I saw him at
church, he would come up to me and ask if I needed a hug. This was
so special to me, and I was grateful for this sensitive young man.

On Wednesday, February 17th, the Temple clothing we had ordered
for Si arrived from Calgary. Jim Mason, Eltie, Marinus, and I went to
the funeral home and dressed Si in his white clothes and his beautiful
Temple robes. He looked like a royal prince. My heart was so full of
love and gratitude for this valiant son. What a sacred privilege it was to
be able to dress him, this last time, in the robes of the Holy Priesthood.
After we finished dressing him, Marinus offered a beautiful prayer.
The spirit was so strong and I know that Si was there with us.

John Livingstone — the Director of the Church Education System
for Saskatchewan — brought over a dozen copies of the Book of
Mormon. I wrote Si's testimony in them and put a picture of him in
each one as well. Marinus and I then took three of them to the ICU
and gave them to the people that Si had asked me to give them to. I
know Si was happy that we kept our promise to him..

Dr. Gibbings and the nurses in the ICU were so kind to us. Dr.
Gibbings hugged us both.

We then left for Edmonton.

The next evening, we went to Frank and Jen's for dinner and then
to the South Side Memorial Chapel for a family viewing. All of my children were there. Leigh Ann came from Toronto and Barb came from
Provo. Two of Marinus' daughters — Kathy and Renee — also came.

Si's good friend, Ken Pollock, and my very close friends, Diane and Derrel Hudson were also there.

Because Si was so swollen and didn't look like himself, some of the children chose not to look at him. I think they wished to remember him at his best. When I looked at him I saw that his body bore the testimony of his suffering, of his pain, and the frailty of this earthly existence. I also saw that he had borne it all with grace and honour. He looked so very beautiful to me.

Jen had picked out a lovely memorial book for Si and everyone signed it. She and Marinus had both been so helpful in looking after the arrangements for Frank and me. I was very grateful for them both.

43

THE FUNERAL

Si's funeral was held on Friday, February 19, 1993 at 2:00 p.m. in the Whyte Avenue Chapel in Edmonton.

We put up a display of pictures of Si, copies of articles he had written, and copies of the Book of Mormon for people to take. While we were setting it up, Jacquie Champion came in and handed me the most beautiful painting of the Alberta Temple. She had painted it the day Si passed away. She had also written a wonderful poem about Si called 'Young Prince' that she had taped to the back of the picture. What a wonderful and priceless gift this was. I shall always cherish it.

Before we took Si's casket into the chapel for the service, we gathered as a family and Kent offered a most beautiful family prayer.

Over 300 people attended the funeral. All of the copies of the Book of Mormon were taken. Two ladies came up to me after the funeral, with tears running down their faces, clutching the Book of Mormon, and promised me that they would read it. How happy my Si must have been. He loved the Book of Mormon so very much and received great joy from sharing it with others. I know that Si's missionary work will continue and the harvest will be rich.

The funeral service was beautiful and I was truly grateful that so many members of Si's family were willing and able to participate in it. I feel that it was a great help to each of us in the healing of our sorrow. One minute we were all crying, and the next minute we were all laughing as we shared the wonderful experiences we each had had with Si. It was a beautiful celebration of his life. I am sure that all who were there were touched by the spirit that was there, and will desire to keep that spirit with them always. Many of the patients and staff from the Aberhart came, as well as some of our neighbours from Lendrum. Frank and Jen's neighbours, and staff from Frank's office were also there. The outpouring of love and friendship we felt was overwhelming.

Our former Bishop and close friend, Derrell Hudson, conducted the funeral.

Bishop Hank Takahashi's Remarks

We saw him grow, we saw him struggle, and yet he was able to do much. The family will mourn the loss of Si because he has been the center of their lives for 18 years, and they have done much to help him achieve his goals.

It is surprising to me that he survived these 18 years for some of the tricks he played on his mother. I'll tell you one more. One day his mother walked into the hospital and every one looked so somber. Si's door was closed. When she opened it, the room was dark. A sheet was pulled over Si's head. She rushed over to him thinking the worst, pulled back the sheet and what was he doing?! Laughing!! That's the kind of person Si was. Although he was paralyzed, he didn't lose his sense of humor.

Si had a firm testimony that Jesus is the Christ, and that someday he would see his Redeemer. He studied the scriptures. He was able to master the use of his computer to a point where he could write down his thoughts.

He continued his school education to a point where he was in his grade 12 year. His life did not end just because he was confined. We used to bring him out where we played ball, and he was one of the coaching staff there. He enjoyed that; in fact I remember watching him one day as the ball was hit and it went up in the air and we watched it come down to where Si was as if he had a glove on and was going to catch it. We were all afraid it was going to hit him, but he didn't flinch! He enjoyed that.

He was a fellow that, although he couldn't move, he was able to reach out to those about him and make everybody feel a little better because they were alive and they were able to do things.

My prayer is that the blessings of the Lord will be with all of us that we will gain from what he has taught us that — Jesus is the Christ, of which he bore testimony many times, and that we can live in the Eternal Kingdom together as a family. I pray the Lord will be with us as we hope for that great and glorious day, in the name of Jesus Christ, amen.

Ben's talk

In the past few days since Si's passing, I have reflected upon his life. I would like to share a few memories that I have. Since I was very young at the time of his accident, being only 8 years old, my memories of Si are quite limited before that time. I remember that Si had a great love of music. He would literally spend hours playing the piano. I remember sitting with him in his room in the basement listening to old 45's and pleading with him that the next time he was at the store, he would buy me my own copy. He never did. Si enjoyed drawing and was really a fantastic cartoonist and through his influence and my trying to emulate him, I discovered a talent for drawing in myself. Si loved food! I've never seen anyone eat the way he did. A typical snack consisted of a box of cereal and a carton of milk. He'd just fill a salad bowl and eat the whole thing in one sitting. Si also had a great love for sports. Mostly the only reason I knew this was because it seemed like he was always hurt. He always had something bandaged up, an ankle or a knee. Si was very competitive. I remember always having contests with him sitting at the kitchen table, each with a package of soda crackers, and just cramming them into our mouths to see who could eat them all first. Si and I had many bike races. He would always give me a block head start and I remember one time, I was racing along and looking back to see how fast he was gaining on me only to see his handlebars come separated from the bike and him spreading himself all over the road. The only thing he said to me was, "Don't tell Mom." She found out anyways because he completely tore up his back and bled quite badly.

I do vividly remember that Si was a really bad driver. Whenever he was behind the wheel, Mom pretty much spent the whole time screaming. There was a certain degree of terror always involved. One time we were travelling to southern Alberta. Si was driving, Mom was sleeping, and Si just about planted us head first into a semi-trailer. He would have if it wasn't for a bit of inspiration on Mom's part. She just suddenly woke up and grabbed the steering wheel. It is my belief that part of the reason Si has spent the last 18 years paralyzed was for our protection.

Mostly, I remember Si as the big guy who lived downstairs. Even though I was small for my age, he seemed impossibly tall. At 16, he was well over 6 feet tall. Quite often we would comment when lifting Si into bed, as 3 of us were struggling to do this, how much easier it would have been if I had broken my neck instead of Si.

I have related some of these memories because I have tried this week to remember Si as he was before his accident. Because the next time I see Si, he won't be flat on his back, confined to a wheelchair. He will be standing straight. He will be healthy, and I know I will still have to look him squarely in the chest.

My memories of Si since the time of his accident are very much different. I learned of a spirit, a will to live, and a sense of humour that in my experience, have never been equalled.

Soon after Si's accident, Si and my Mom had a conversation that shows the essence of the type of person Si is. Since Si was such an active, dynamic person, my Mom worried about how Si would react to the reality that in this life, he would never walk again, never play vol-leyball, or run, or play the piano. When she asked him what he would do now, he thought for a moment and replied, "Mom, I did the best I could at those things when I did them. Now I will just do something else." And he did just that.

Si loved to learn. At the time of his accident, he was half way through the eleventh grade. He set out to continue his education and was almost able to finish his Grade 12. It was a long and tedious process and surprising, his marks took on dramatic improvements. He achieved 90 in Chemistry and 85 in Biology and a 75 in Math.

Si later on focused on computers and the scriptures. He read through the entire Standard Works multiple times and could quote verses extensively.

Si had patience that I think could only be equalled by that great man Job. Si endured pain and discomfort, the depths of which few have experienced. Through all of it, he remained positive and cheerful. His acceptance of his situation and his limitations was remarkable. He also accepted our limitations and our fears when dealing with him. No one could read his lips like Mom. The rest of us really struggled when it came to communicating with him — me included. One time, he was trying to tell me something. After several minutes and no success, I asked him to spell the word. Now Si's incredible intelligence is only bested by his awful spelling. After several minutes, I had the letters R A Y S I R. After some more puzzling, I finally figured out that he wanted his electric shaver or 'razor'. The whole process took over half an hour.

Si had a fantastic sense of humour and constantly told jokes, made plays on words, and was a serious practical joker. Mom, much to my enjoyment and everyone else's, was usually Si's primary victim.

It is a tradition at LDS funerals to share something about the Plan of Salvation. I am grateful I can share some thoughts with you on this most important subject. It is important that it is conveyed to you why Si had such a love of life and why Si in his extreme physically restricted condition, was such a happy, outgoing individual.

In the beginning, before the earth was created, we all existed as spirit entities. We lived with our Father in Heaven as his family. He, as our Father, we as His children. We wanted to be like Him. He, as a perfected, glorified individual, had a body of flesh and bones. We existed only as spirits. So our Father set forth a plan whereby we could come down to this earth, take up these mortal, physical bodies and prove ourselves worthy to return to His presence. In due course, the earth, having been created, our first parents, Adam and Eve, were placed in the Garden of Eden. (Genesis 2:7) Soon after, the Lord gave a commandment to Adam (Genesis 2:16-17). Through the events that were to follow, the stage was set whereby the entire human family would have entrance to the world. Satan tempted Eve and beguiled her and she did eat of the fruit and gave also to her husband and he did eat. Because they partook of the forbidden fruit, some very important changes were wrought. Firstly, the world and everything in it became mortal. Adam and Eve, now mortal beings, became subject to infirmities both in mind and in body. Pain, sickness, and physical death were now a part of life. Secondly, Adam and Eve were now commanded to leave the Garden of Eden and being shut out from the presence of God, suffered spiritual death. These stages of physical and spiritual death are the conditions under which you and I are born and now live in the world. Thankfully, our Father in Heaven, in his infinite wisdom and love, included in His wonderful plan, a Saviour and a Redeemer to overcome the effects of the fall of Adam. In the meridian of time, Jesus the Christ, the only begotten Son of God, through His sufferings in the Garden of Gethsemane and upon the cross, took upon himself the sins of all generations of the human family. He did this, however, with a condition. Since we are responsible for the manner in which we live our lives, His sacrifice will only pay for our sins if we believe in Him, if we repent, and change and seek to live righteously.

Since Adam brought death into the world and with death, came every degree of physical pain and imperfection, and since we have no control over the fact that we die, redemption from death has been made a free gift to all. Jesus Christ, through His death and resurrection, made it possible that everyone that has ever lived or will ever live upon the earth will take up this mortal frame and live again. (D&C 19)

When Si died, and when we die, our spirits and our body separate. Just as Si's body lays here before us made up of the dust of the earth, without the life of a spirit, will return to dust. But the spirit lives on, conscious, thinking and active. I know that Si, just as he did in this life, still has a very important work to perform, and I am sure that he will be put to work just as soon as someone catches up with him. At some point hence, the spirit and the body will again be reunited, resurrected to a perfected and immortal state, free of pain, sickness and sin, never to die again. (Alma 11). Si had a very strong testimony of this. I know that even though he didn't dwell on it, Si looked forward to the day when his mortal would put on immortality and when his corruption would put on incorruption.

Through all of Si's physical afflictions and limitations, he never let it affect his outlook that life is worth living. He never wasted a moment or an opportunity to learn or to share. He showed me that living the

Gospel is where pure and lasting joy is found. He showed me that developing the mind and the spirit is of most worth. He helped me gain an appreciation for the scriptures and the life of Jesus Christ. I feel I would let Si down if I didn't challenge and encourage each of you to read the Book of Mormon. If you don't have one, get one. Read it and pray to our Father in Heaven to learn of its truthfulness. Si would want you to do this. Si was an inspiration to everyone he came in contact with. He inspired me, and I am extremely grateful that Si is my brother. I look forward to being with him again and continuing our relationship and friendship. In closing, I would like to share a scripture from the words of Isaiah.

"And he will destroy in this mountain the face of the covering cast over all people, and the vail that is spread over all nations.

He will swallow up death in victory; and the Lord God will wipe away tears from all faces; and the rebuke of his people shall he take away from off all the earth: for the Lord God has spoken it." Isaiah 25: 7, 8.

I say these things in the name of Jesus Christ, Amen.

David's Talk

Si was a character right from the getgo. His name is a derivative of my father's grandfather's surname — Siedel, and Si is a rather easy name to spell- Si. Not that difficult. But Si, when he got to Grade one decided that his name was 'Is', so his homework and what-not came home with the name 'Is' on it. Actually there were some things that I typed up about Si very late last night and even though I spell checked it, I'm embarrassed now to see some mistakes so I think that it was Si that typed it up.

I don't want you to think that Benjie said everything that I'm going to say, but he did. Fortunately though, the memories that Benjie has are very much the same as the memories I have about Si and they are all very positive. I'm going to delve into a little bit more detail though because I'm older.

Benjie mentioned that Si was obviously very athletic and that he was. If any of you have ever visited our home in Lendrum, the roof is very high. We have these beams that come down from the ceiling and the big thrill for Si was to jump up and touch the beam, and he could do that with regularity. I found it to be a bit of a challenge. Of course I was considerably smaller than he was and so sometimes he would pick me up and let me touch the roof.

Si had a wonderful sense of humour and he often enjoyed pulling gags on my Mom and on anybody else that he could trick. A favorite of his was that he would get into the car, before my Mom would, and turn everything on. He would turn the radio up full blast, the wipers, the lights, he would turn everything on. My mom would start the car and of course it would go off like a siren. She didn't know where to start turning things off. When she pushed the channel button on the radio, she found he had every channel locked into his favorite station.

Mom was always losing her keys so one time for Christmas, Si bought a present for my mom which was a very large key ring that said "If you lose this...forget it!" He wrapped it in a small box and then a bigger box and then in several even bigger boxes until it was in this huge box which my Mom thought was some big present. He taped candy bars on some of the layers to give her strength to get through it.

Quite often, when Si was in the hospital, we unfortunately couldn't control his temperature very well and one time when I was there he thought that he was cold and he asked me to cover him up and I said, "Si, it's really warm in here. I don't think you need a blanket." He said, "Look, if you don't cover me up, I'm going to turn into a Si-cicle!"

Most people that knew Si before his accident recall that he could play the piano. He would quite often go to the youth dances, but these dances weren't just dances for him. They were recitals! He could often be found off in one of the rooms, wherever a piano was, playing, and often times there would be more people in with him than in the dance. My mother's Aunt Augusta, before she died, made Si promise that when he passed on that he would come and play Crocodile Rock for her, and I'm sure that is just what he did.

Si had an incredible gift of drawing. I wish Keith Salmon was here. Keith was one of Si's caricatures and he called him Super Salmon and he'd always draw him eating bowls of kelp — 'Kelp, the breakfast of Salmons'. He had, I guess, a demented sense of humour that he got from the Mad comic books. I don't know if any of you have seen it but he would always draw that Alfred E. Newman guy. I think there's an example of it out in the cultural hall, you should have a look at it.

Si was rather injury prone and I had either the fortune or misfortune of being present most of the time when he got hurt. Sometimes I was responsible. Of course I wouldn't admit that at the time. One time I threw a football for him and he dove for it and he either cracked or broke his collarbone and he tried to beat me up afterwards but he couldn't because he was too injured.

He loved to skate and quite often we'd go down to the rink in Lendrum and skate. At the time, back in the old days, they had this thing that would go in front of your face to protect your teeth in case you fell, and because our Dad was a dentist he was quite happy for us to wear it. One day Si decided he didn't want to wear it and, of course, that time he fell face first on to the ice and chipped out his two front teeth. I was there. He had numerous black eyes. He slammed his fingers in the front door of the church and he had numerous accidents in the cultural hall playing basketball. While playing one day, as he was rebounding a ball, somebody hit him on the top of his head and he bit his tongue almost through. One time at school he was walking past a plate glass window when it fell and he tried to catch it. Of course it cut his fingers all up. Another time, he was riding his bike with pop bottles. He was going to take them down and get money for them and he wiped out on his bike and ground his hand into the broken glass. Benjie already mentioned about other times he wiped out on his bike.

Si and money were easily parted. He would get his allowance and it was gone. He would buy records or he would buy candy or he would buy whatever but he never had money. It was the same deal when we would go on family vacations. Si would buy stuff right away and I would go up to him and say, "Si does that taste good?" And he would say, "Here, have a bite". I would take a bite and at the end of the trip, I still had all my money. Mom says I still have the first nickel she ever gave me!

As Benjie mentioned as well, my mom always claimed that he had a hollow leg — at least one, maybe two. Quite often he would get up from the dinner table and immediately go to the cupboard and make a peanut butter sandwich. I could never figure that one out, but he was obviously a very big, hungry boy.

One of the fondest memories I have of Si was when we were quite young — in fact, Benjie was just born — and we didn't like to go to bed even though our parents liked us to go to bed early, so we often got into trouble. We would be up on the bunk beds and jump off of them and do all sorts of crazy stuff. We tried to think of something to keep us from getting into trouble, so Si devised this little trick. He tied a string to the doorknob and a string to the light switch and then we went on playing. Of course, my Dad heard us up there because we were creating quite a ruckus. He came up ready to lay into us, ripped the door open, the light flipped off, we were in bed, he laughed and we didn't get into trouble.

If Si were here, I guess this would be more of a roast than anything.

The main thing that I want to say is that Si was a wonderful brother. I learned a lot from him. He was an inspiration to me, and just as he lifted me up so I could touch those beams, he lifted me and others up by his example. I am so thankful to him for the example he has set as my big brother.

I say these things in the name of Jesus Christ, Amen.

Frank's Talk

I may have a great deal of trouble getting through this today. I hope you bear with me.

Si was more to me than a son. I always felt like we were sort of fellow comedians in the comedy we call life. Benjie told you, and David told you about the way Si got his name. It is a grand old German name, Frank Siedel. My grandfather was called Old Si, my brother Hal was called Little Si and my son, who was supposed to be Si, became Is. And I don't know whether or not his humour was that well developed at that young age, but it seemed to be.

Si was to me a totally unique individual. In fact, so are the rest of my kids. But what made him so unique were the challenges that he was faced with so early in life. In one brief instant of time, he suffered probably the most horrific disability that anybody could have. I remember that time so well. As I left that volleyball practice, I saw him shooting baskets and a thought flashed through my mind — Si is fearless. I used to tell him when we were playing volleyball, "Si, you don't have to go through the wall to get a ball. I mean, if you don't get that point, the world won't cave in." He was just fearless. I guess that's the best way to describe him. But in that brief instant of time, he became a person who functioned with only his mind. He developed a talent for humour and I think that talent made the people around him much more comfortable with his condition. A lot of people are very afraid or they don't feel comfortable around people with disabilities, but Si didn't make you feel that way.

On his 10th birthday, we were traveling in two cars to go to Trail, BC, and we were going through Montana. We were traveling in two cars because we had Anita's mother and her stepfather with us. But since Si was involved, something was bound to happen. So it turned out that in Browning, Montana, on his 10th birthday, we decided to stop and have something to eat. When we finished eating, we came out and, of course, Si was in the bathroom and we left without him. We drove for about three hours before we finally stopped and discovered that Si was not with us. And Si, in that time, could have been any place in the world. The three hours spent driving back to Browning were just terrible for us but we were finally reunited with him. When we arrived in Trail, BC we went into a restaurant to have something to eat. As we were leaving the restaurant, Si again had to go to the bathroom so we thought we would walk out to the entryway and wait for him. As I was walking, I felt someone beside me and it was Si and he said, "Dad, don't leave me this time, okay?"

Si became sort of the king of one-liners and I wish with all my heart that I had written them all down. He could play on words to amuse you and astound you. One day, I got to the hospital and the nurse was laughing and I said, "What's going on?" and she said, "Well I was just talking to your son and complimenting him on his smile and what beautiful teeth he has and he said, "Well I should...I see my dentist three or four times a week!"

As I was trying to put this together last night, I thought I was never amused by anyone so much as my son. I'll never forget the faces that he made when his mother would try to kiss him goodnight. He really did have more use of his facilities than just to smile because he would screw that face around like he was going through the worst punishment in the whole world.

Some of the fond memories I have of Si are in the summer months when I would go to see him and we would get him into his chair and we would go out and walk around the university area. One day we came to a statue of abstract art made of pieces of metal welded together. Si had a sense of the arts that I'm sure was more sophisticated than some. I looked at the object and said to him, "Gee, that's quite a beautiful welded piece of art," and he said, "It looks like a welded piece of junk to me!" I knew he had a better sense of the arts than I have!

It was a beautiful glorious day out that day, and I tipped Si's chair back and said, "Si, look up at that beautiful sky." At that particular moment, a group of birds were flying overhead and one deposited a projectile very close to Si's face and he turned to me said, "Do I have to keep looking up?"

Because Si did not have the use of his vocal chords, we needed to read his lips to understand what he was saying. I couldn't read his lips very well. His mother could, but I couldn't. I don't know...it was just something that I could never do very well. And so we used to play this little game. If I couldn't get the word he was trying to tell me, I would have him spell it out. Although his spelling did improve in the latter part of his life, Si was unfortunately, the most horrific speller you could ever imagine, so Si and I were almost incommunicado.

He also had some funny little things that he used to do that, at the time, I found so annoying. I would visit him at night and when it was time for me to leave I would say to him, "Si, I'm really tired tonight. Could you please just tell me now what you want me to do for you while I'm here?" He wouldn't say too much and then as I was getting ready to leave, he'd say, "Dad, can you rewind that tape for me? Dad, could you do this? Dad, could you do that?" and I would get so ticked off at him. But I would walk out of that hospital and think to myself — "How could I be ticked off at someone who had the limited abilities that he had."

He was such an interesting individual to me. I really loved him. I still love him. I'd really like to thank Jen and all my kids for helping me get through this. I want all my kids to know that, even though your mother and I spent a lot of time with Si, we love you all the same.

I'd really like to thank Marinus and Anita today. They improved the quality of Si's life to such a point that I used to call him 'Super quad'. He did have a life that probably not many people in his condition have had or will ever have because they made Si a part of everything they did. I think that shows a wonderful quality of Marinus — that Si was truly his son.

I spent more time with Si than I will ever spend with any one of my children, all of them put together, and yet I hope that they don't resent that (and I'm sure they don't) because as I said before, I feel in my heart the same about all of them.

Last Monday, when Si passed away, I am sure there was a substantial increase in the quantity and the quality of heavenly humour because he certainly did have that attribute.

I have admired many people in my life — my associates that I have worked with, my buddies that I play golf with, my family, my wife Jen, Anita and Marinus and many other people that I have come in contact with. I really admire you all but I must admit, I have only one hero and it is my Si-guy.

My talk

What a wonderful celebration of Si's life this service has been today. It is such a privilege and an honour for me to have this opportunity to pay my tribute to this beautiful son, brother and friend.

I have always said that I must have done something pretty special in the Spirit World to have been chosen to be Si's mom. I love him so very much and I have learned much from him as I have watched him accept, with patience and faith, all the trials of his life and do everything in his power to make the most of his life.

To me, Si's life is a composite of all the attributes of the Gospel. The past 18 years, since his accident happened, have been ones filled with great trials and tribulations, but they have also been filled with great spiritual blessings.

Some of the trials that he has had to endure besides being totally paralysed from his chin down are:

He suffered a stroke, duodenal ulcers, severe kidney stones, two complete kidney failures, two out-of-body experiences, torment from evil spirits, terrible seizures, severe spasms which caused shortness of breath, and large ulcers on his hips and back.

He not only endured all of this but he endured it well, with patience, and faith, and a quiet acceptance of whatever was handed to him. His trials truly became his stepping stones to eternity.

He said that the thing that helped him most in his acceptance of his very limited abilities and to endure his trials, was the knowledge he had of the purpose of life — that this life is only a very small part of eternity, but a very important part. He knew that how he lived here would determine where and how he would spend the whole rest of eternity.

Si had a great love for people, and this love took away his fear. His greatest joy came from sharing his most precious possession — his knowledge of the Gospel — with others. He saw his world as a field that was white, already to harvest, and he thrust in his sickle with all of his might. He seized any opportunity that he could to give away copies of the Book of Mormon. He truly loved this great book and received great strength from the beautiful truths found within it and wanted so much to share it with everyone. His last request to me, just hours before his passing, was to give one of the young men, who had worked so hard to help him, a copy of the Book of Mormon. I am happy to say that we did that for Si before we left Regina.

Si realized how precious and how short the time really is that we have here on the earth, and he tried not to waste a minute of it. He filled the hours of his days with worthwhile, uplifting things that had eternal value. He kept a faithful journal on his computer and spent many hours writing his life story. He listened to uplifting music and good books. He had a stick-to-it-tive-ness that was truly amazing. When he was at the Aberhart, he had an IBM computer that he ran with his lip, but when we moved to Regina, he received a new Apple computer from Randy Marsden of Madenta (who invented special software so that handicapped people such as Si could use a computer). Randy said that Si was his inspiration for his inventions. This new computer required Si to learn a whole new technique of running it. He sat at that computer for at least 8 hours a day and worked and struggled until he mastered how to move the cursor on the screen with a stick in his mouth. I have never seen such patience and perseverance as he showed.

I feel that the most important thing that made Si's life so special was that he truly exemplified the pure love of Christ in his life. He had (and has) great love for his Saviour and deep understanding and gratitude for His atonement and resurrection. It hurt Si's spirit whenever he heard anyone use the Lord's name in vain. He refused to watch videos or go to movies if this sacred name was used disrespectfully in them. Si simply had, as Nephi of old, no disposition to do evil.

Si also felt love from the Saviour and many times was helped through tremendous difficulties by the comfort of that love.

He also loved others as Christ loves — purely and unconditionally. He saw only the good in others and loved them for themselves. He found and appreciated the good qualities in everyone he met. He truly was a person without guile.

Just before he passed away, I told him that he was the most faithful, courageous, and valiant person I had ever known and he said to me, "I have received a lot of help, Mom". He always acknowledged the help he received from Heavenly Father, and each of you here, in your own way, has helped Si fulfill this mission he was called to do in a way that I know is pleasing to our Heavenly Father. Thank you for your love, your acceptance, and your friendship that you each have given to him. His life was touched and made richer by your friendship.

I feel that Si would like me to express a special thank you to his other Mom, Jen Peterson, and to his two Dads, Dad P and Dad B, as he called them, and all his brothers and sisters for all the love and support you have given him, and I know that his greatest desire now is to meet you all again in the Celestial Kingdom of our Father.

Si loved music, and one of his favourite tapes was Janice Kapp Perry's musical," My Turn On Earth". In fact, he listened to it so much that the caregivers and I had him put on his headphones. In closing,

I would like to share the words of one of the songs from the tape with you.

I am the one that writes my own story.
I decide the person I'll be.
What goes in the plot and what will not
Is pretty much up to me.

And just in case I need to erase it was figured out before,
A thing called Repentance.
It can wipe out a sentence, a page, a chapter or more.
I am the one that writes my own story
I decide the person I'll be.

Everyone that writes their own story
Now and then will make some mistakes.
But given some care they needn't stay there
And this is all that it takes.
You must know you've done wrong
And so you feel very bad and then
Don't try to hide it, do try to right it
And vow you won't do it again.

I am the one who writes my own story.
I decide the person I'll be.
This book of mine is very important
And so someone is waiting right there
To help with my story,
He's been there before me,
And is always as close as a prayer.
We will write each day and night
And do it well and faithfully.
A wonderful story of sadness
And glory is written by Jesus and me.

I am the one that writes my own story.
I decide the person I'll be.

Si truly did write a wonderful story of sadness and glory and it was indeed written by his Saviour and him. I say these things in the name of Jesus Christ, Amen.

On Saturday, February 20th, we traveled to Raymond for the burial service. Si was buried at the Temple Hill Cemetery. Many of my relatives that live in southern Alberta were there. Marinus dedicated the grave. He gave a beautiful heartfelt prayer. It was a bitterly cold day, but our hearts were warm from the outpouring of love we felt from those around us. Si was buried at the feet of my Uncle Alvin and Aunt Augusta Bullock and beside my Grandma and Grandpa Bullock.

After the burial, we all gathered at the Raymond Stake Center and the sisters from Lori's ward, served a wonderful meal to us.

44

THE MEMORIAL SERVICE

A Memorial service was held for Si in Regina on Friday, February 26th. Several people gave wonderful talks at this service as well. I am including the ones that I was given copies of.

Marinus' Talk

Si has touched the lives of many people, and he has touched these lives in many different ways. I had the privilege of coming into Si's life in 1978, when Anita and I were married. Right from the beginning, he started calling me Dad B. I never became very good at reading his lips, but I have been greatly blessed by being the recipient of his brilliant wit and great spirit. Never have I seen a human being as determined to live and fight during times of illness as this valiant and magnificent son of ours.

With the invention of the personal computer and inventions of special software and hardware by Peter Nelson of the Canadian National Research Council in Ottawa, Randy Marsden of Madenta in Edmonton and others, Si, with a little bit of help, mastered the technology and he used to say to me many times, "Thanks to everyone, I now have a voice".

It is my belief that Si loved everyone. Si's physical body was paralyzed from the chin down, he was not even able to move his head, or speak out loud. His life of paralysis was changed into a life of service. One of our church leaders coined the phrase, 'Do It'. Si lived that motto!

He had no difficulty in asking others to assist him in doing the things he could not do for himself. He studied long hours, and obtained great wisdom and learning about things that really mattered.

He was, and is, a friend to all, especially the physically ill, the emotionally troubled, the socially inept. He also counselled with those in need of succour. He avoided evil and gently reprimanded those who abused the name of his Saviour and friend, Jesus Christ.

Children admired his wheelchair and were not afraid to show their childlike interest in his condition, and he always greeted them with a smile. Young people and adults received inspiration from him. The Saviour, Jesus Christ, loved and comforted him, preserved his life, and, during the early hours of Monday, February 15, 1993, allowed our son and brother Si to use his agency to return home.

I know that Si lives. I miss you, Si. I know that Jesus Christ lives and that through His resurrection, we will all be resurrected and live again. In the name of Jesus Christ, amen.

Jim Mason's Talk

(Jim and his wife, Aldean, and their children, Amber and Kyle, were very close friends to Si while he lived in Regina.)

"We sing an inspiring song in which we say, "I walked today where Jesus walked". Wouldn't it be a thrilling experience if on some beautiful day, we could stand on that spot of ground where Jesus stood. That wasn't practical for Si, but Si's actions were practical and even more important, Si strove to think about what Jesus thought. He read and listened to tapes to absorb His every idea. Si lived as He lived and did as He did. Si showed us by his example that we can be what Jesus wants us to become by doing what He wants us to do. One of the most important powers in the world is the power of example. Carlyle said, "We reform others when we walk uprightly".

Joseph Fielding Smith said, "No righteous man is ever taken before his time. In the case of the faithful, they are simply transferred to other fields of labour. The Lord's work goes on". Si prepared well, for he is now about his Father's work. I know he was here to become like our eternal Heavenly Father. I believe Si would look back at his mortal experience as this unknown poet did.

> *Pain stayed so long, I said to him today,*
> *"I will not have you with me anymore."*
> *I stomped my foot and said, "Be on your way".*
> *Then paused there, startled by the look he wore.*
> *"I, who have been your friend," he said to me.*
> *"I, who have been your teacher. All you know*
> *Of understanding, love and sympathy*
> *And patience, I have taught you*
> *Shall I go?"*
> *He spoke the truth, this strange, unwanted guest.*
> *I watched him leave and knew that he was wise.*
> *He left a heart made tender in my breast.*
> *He left a clearer vision in my eyes.*
> *I dried my tears and lifted up a song*
> *Even for one who tortured me so long.*

But Si was also here to touch and change our lives as well. Each of our circumstances is unique to me and you alone. Each must practise the thoughts and acts of our own character. Si's selflessness touched me deeply. Through his service to others, Si demonstrated his relationship and intimacy with the Saviour. E.g. — his sense of humour put me at ease with him — his patience when I couldn't understand what he was saying. — his tolerance when I took too long to get the word he was saying and he would have forgotten it. — often we would read together and he would insist that it was time to write his testimony in yet another Book of Mormon. — his example of keeping the Lord's work foremost. — that last night when Aldean visited he remarked that he had some more copies of the Book of Mormon to place.

I learned from Si that selflessness is the only way in Heaven and on Earth whereby we can be sanctified. Every requirement of God's plan for our salvation places upon us the responsibility of giving of ourselves. In the spirit of selflessness, men and women share themselves, their talents and their means in benevolent service to mankind and to God. I know their reward is the freeing of their souls, the growth of their love, their nearness to divinity, their worthiness of the companionship of the spirit. Robert Ingersoll said at his brother's funeral, "If everyone to whom he did some loving service should bring a blossom to his grave, he would sleep tonight beneath a wilderness of flowers". And so it was for Si. He touched the lives of many.

I often wondered what Whistler's mother was thinking about as she sat in that rocking chair. A poem captures part of what she might be thinking.

And now as evening shadows gather
About to fade off into gloom
A mother sits alone, pose serene, husband gone, children gone, the work
is done, twilight comes.
She thinks of the past in gratitude
And gazes wistfully out into the future unafraid.

I love this Anita — Si's mother who loved him into being, whose loving arms sustained him, whose unfaltering faith and appreciation encouraged him to do and to become. Anita has been his wisest critic, his best friend, his mother. I've come to understand a mother's love — a Christ-like love, and I am grateful, for now I appreciate my own mother all the more.

Sister Grassley of the General Primary Presidency was at our last Tanner Encampment. We were all impressed by her vitality and her love of the youth. Several of us were struck by Brother Grassley's quiet, unobtrusive support. He smoothed the way before her, gave her praise and encouragement and picked up behind her. Striking, you bet — but another example of this is close at hand.

I love my brother Marinus. From him, I have come to understand what our Father expects when we are to sustain our companions. He smoothes the way, gives support, counsels. I've come to understand what our Heavenly Father expects of me as husband and helpmate.

How have Si and this loving vital family touched my life? Profoundly! What to do? We are afforded time for contemplation, for evaluation, and for some strong resolutions as to how we might better prepare our own lives. This is the challenge Si gives each of us. In the name of Jesus Christ, Amen.

All of the talks given and the beautiful music that was rendered helped to make these two services a truly wonderful celebration of Si's life.

A beautiful poem was written by Jacquie Champion on the day Si passed away. It was read at the beginning of Si's funeral, and I thought it would be a fitting end to this story of his life.

YOUNG PRINCE

I care not for the trappings and gold of earthly realms;
Nor do the heirs of pewter thrones impress.
The titled honours of the throng
Are hollow to my seeking humbled mind.
Of royalty the world seems sadly wrong.
When elevated birth-dictated crowns
Parade their fabled ways in pomp and pride,
Trumpeted by blaring song.
But of a prince
I do know one...
Whose dignity and royal soul surpass
The purple velvet and the shrieking brass.
His Father is the King of Kings;
His Brother's crown of thorns, worn for us all.
Triumphant, proven, noble, now at rest.
Dear Si, my friend, a prince, the very best.

Si is gone — but it is my hope and prayer that his 'legacy of faith' will live on in our hearts forever.

EPILOGUE

When Si's accident first happened, I didn't have any idea how he would react to going from a healthy young man to a complete quadriplegic, and it is still hard for me to believe the great faith and courage he had. Not once did he rail against what had happened to him or blame his Heavenly Father. Maybe he was being strong for me, I don't know, but I am so grateful for the example he was of all I had tried to teach him, and so much more.

As I look back on his life, I feel that there were three major principles that were key to his being able to be strong and faithful through all the difficult circumstances that he went through, during the almost eighteen years he spent as a quadriplegic..

These principles are:

1. We must come to know who we really are in relationship to our Heavenly Father, our Saviour and our fellow human beings. Si knew who he was — a son of God — and he had complete trust in our Heavenly Father's plan for his life. He also knew who everyone else was — also children of that same Heavenly Father. This knowledge helped him to be able to look beyond the outward appearance or behaviour of another person and see the real person inside — the spirit child of God within. Because of this knowledge, many of his closest friends were some of our Heavenly Father's less fortunate children (at least in the eyes of the world). They felt comfortable with him and accepted by him. Their spirits just seemed to grow under his unconditional love and they came to more fully know who they really were.

2. We must have complete faith and trust in our Heavenly Father's plan for our lives as it relates to the purpose of life. We must understand the great purpose of trials and tribulations in that plan, remembering that we are spiritual beings here on earth to have mortal experiences.

3. We must realize that every commandment, law, principle, and council given to us by our Heavenly Father (through His prophets) is for our happiness and to help us on our journey back to Him. They are given to us because He loves us and wants us to return to Him.

These three principles made a great difference in the way Si accepted the paralysis and the completely different life he was called to live. He couldn't change his situation, but he could certainly choose how he reacted to it. He chose to not see himself as a victim. He actually thanked his Heavenly Father every day for the trials he had to bear. He was grateful for the opportunities for growth that they gave him.

CPSIA information can be obtained at www.ICGtesting.com
Printed in the USA
LVOW11s0111040915

452607LV00002B/98/P